FLOWER FESTIVALS
Themes and Ideas

FRANCES PARKINSON

Foreword by Ronald Blythe
Illustrations by Wilda Woodland

DAVID & CHARLES
Newton Abbot   London   North Pomfret (Vt)

British Library Cataloguing in Publication Data

Parkinson, Frances
. Flower festivals: themes and ideas.
1. Flower arrangement in churches
I. Title
745.92'6   SB449.5.C4
ISBN 0–7153–8745–6

Photoset by
Northern Phototypesetting Co, Bolton
and printed in Great Britain
by Redwood Burn Ltd, Trowbridge
for David & Charles Publishers plc
Brunel House, Newton Abbot, Devon

Published in the United States of America
by David & Charles Inc
North Pomfret, Vermont 05053, USA

Contents

	Foreword by Ronald Blythe	5
	Introduction	6
	Acknowledgements	7
1	The Purpose of Flowers in Church	9
2	The Planning	17
3	The Places	26
4	Hymns	44
5	Poetry with Flowers	48
6	Wedding Flowers	54
7	Church Services	59
8	Flowers in Variety	68
9	The Crafts of 'Your' Town	72
10	The Language of Flowers	79
11	Famous Sayings	84
12	God's Garden	89
13	The Seasons	94
14	Your Town's Clubs	98
15	Wild Flowers	105
16	Church Festivals	108
17	The Arts	116
18	Dried Flowers	124
19	The Church's Year and the Church's Week	128
20	'Things of Joy'	135
	Conclusion	138
	A Table of Liturgical Colours	139
	Old English Table of Flowers	141
	Bibliography	144

This book is dedicated to all those with whom I have shared the pleasure of decorating our little church with flowers.

'Who of men can tell
that flowers would bloom
or that green fruit would swell.'

Keats

Foreword

Flowers have provided their own special symbolism for Christianity from its origin to the present. Plants of all kinds have long been part of the liturgical year, their natural calendar and the Church's calendar being, for centuries, coordinated as the cycle of worship passes through the seasons. Inside and out, church buildings are covered with patterns suggested by leaves, petals and branches, whilst the actual blooms for Easter, Christmas, etc are placed on the altar, the place of life, and the grave, the place of death. To come across a church without flowers (or worse half-dead and uncared-for flowers) is disconcerting, for we have become accustomed to loving, gifted standards in this respect.

Arranging flowers in churches is quite unlike arranging them in houses or anywhere else. A combination of simplicity and knowledge is required, and also a mixture of taste and feeling. Only someone who has spent half a lifetime 'seeing to the flowers', as we say in the country, in an ancient church would be able to express these requirements – or, indeed, dare to! I cannot think of anyone better qualified to do this than Frances Parkinson whose flowers at Hoo, Suffolk, have long been both an education and a delight where I am concerned. Christ saw flowers as forms of earthly perfection, and in her calm, intelligent way Frances Parkinson keeps this concept of them uppermost as she guides and suggests. Her book is a must, not only for all those whose names make up the rotas on countless church doors, but for anyone who sees flowers in a church as a spiritual necessity.

RONALD BLYTHE

Introduction

For some time I have felt that there is a need for some rationalisation concerning the purpose of flower festivals. Visiting flower festivals has become a regular event during spring and summer weekends. In some cases as many people enter the doors of a country church over the period of a flower festival as do for the rest of the Sundays in the year put together. How important it is, therefore, that we give visitors a spiritual message as well as the pleasure afforded by the flowers themselves.

When a new musical is staged, it is not enough that the first-night audience is spellbound with the glamour and glitter of it all. If it is to be a 'hit' then they must be humming the tunes the next day, and the next week, and ultimately they may buy the record.

Many people have told me that they find the choice of a theme particularly difficult, and it is for this reason that I started to write this book. Fundamentally it is a book of ideas which I hope may be of help to the reader.

The ideas I put forward are equally applicable to all Christian denominations, just as history is common to all. I trust, however, that readers will make allowance for the fact that, as a member of the Church of England, I have used examples from the form of service best known to me. This is certainly not intended to be the only approach, and I hope that those of other persuasions will make the necessary adjustments to their own needs and traditions.

In no way is this intended to be a book on flower arranging. It is my firm belief that flower arrangement should be a very natural thing and its execution very personal: however, if books are needed, there are many beautiful ones to choose from.

FRANCES PARKINSON

Acknowledgements

It is with very sincere gratitude that I acknowledge the help given to me by many friends.

I would like specifically to refer firstly to my husband and also to my family for their encouragement and support, and in particular to my daughters for their helpful reading of the scripts.

To Wilda Woodland who has worked so hard over all the drawings I am extremely grateful. She has produced not only exactly what I wanted but has done so with great patience and a sense of humour which has made, for me, our working together so enjoyable. I do not claim to have grown all the flowers used in the various arrangements; I am well-known for begging bits and pieces from friends, all of whom have been most generous.

The Reverend Horace Wright has, most kindly, been an endless source of information which, without his help, I would never have acquired and I am deeply grateful to him for all the trouble he has taken on my behalf.

My handwriting can be fairly illegible at times and my spelling worse. Phyllis Shaw has patiently deciphered one and corrected the other to type the manuscript most efficiently whilst always managing to persuade me that it was no trouble at all.

Edward Morgan AMPA of Culpho Hall, Ipswich, has most kindly taken the photographs for the jacket as well as recording most of the arrangements in colour prints. It has been a great pleasure to me to witness his technical skill and sympathetic understanding of the subject.

For the generous use of the churches in their care I am indebted to Mrs Dod Rope, Major George Baird, The Reverend Roger Dixon MA and The Reverend Jim Laurie MA.

I am most grateful to Pam Griffiths of David & Charles for guiding me, so patiently and helpfully, through what, for me, was the previously unexplored world of publishing. Finally my greatest debt of gratitude is to Ronald Blythe. Without his constructive criticism, and encouragement, together with the time and trouble he has taken on my behalf, this book would never have been published. I am equally grateful to him for his generous foreword.

My publishers and I are grateful to all those who have given us permission to use copyright material: Mrs Sheila Hooper and Jonathan Cape for extracts from *Kilvert's Diary* edited by William Plomer; Cassell Ltd for extracts from *Brewer's Dictionary of Phrase and Fable* edited by Ivor H. Evans; A. R. Mowbray & Co Ltd for extracts from *The Saints and their Flowers* by Gladys Taylor; Margaret Pickston and Michael Joseph for the poem from *The Language of Flowers*. I have also used extracts from *Flower Arrangement in Church* by Katharine Morrison McClinton published by World's Work. I am indebted for their kind help to The East Suffolk County Library, The Bodleian Library Oxford, and the library of The Royal Horticultural Society.

1 The Purpose of Flowers in Church

Art achieves a purpose which is not its own

Benjamin Constant

The purpose of flowers in church has always been twofold. They were there not only as beautiful and joyous symbols of God's goodness to us, but as outward and visible signs of the individual significance each held in Christian beliefs. These Christian beliefs, in early times, were not divorced from superstition, and flowers, plants and trees were symbols of these superstitions and legends, becoming in the course of time traditions, many of which survive today. The history of the usage of flowers in the Christian church is as fascinating as it is long and must be the subject of another book. What I feel is relevant here is to trace, albeit on the periphery, the purpose of the flowers and plants used in this way.

Herbs were widely used in rites and ceremonies. In addition to their medicinal qualities, they were closely associated with superstition. Hyssop (marjoram or the thorny caper) was a witch repellent, and as such used in services of purification. The medicinal uses of herbs were numerous and, because the church was not only responsible for the spiritual health of its people, but their physical well-being as well, every cathedral and monastery had its own herb garden.

Trees too were associated with superstition and legend; the protective influence of bay trees for example kept away thunder and lightning, while the rowan kept off the Hallowe'en witches. The aspen was said to tremble because the cross for Christ's crucifixion was made of its wood; the elder too is said to have provided wood for the cross; again other sources connected the elder with Judas who, legend has it, hung himself on an elder tree and the mushroom-like excrescences on the bark are still known as 'Judas' ears'. Yet again, he is said to have hung himself from a fig tree. That we shall never know for sure is irrelevant, but what is interesting is the inevitable variation on a theme that one finds in research of this nature when superstition and legend have been passed down through the centuries.

Finally, to the flowers themselves which, as well as greenery, were used so much as to warrant the sacristan often keeping a special garden from which to supply them. The legends attached to flowers are charming and numerous. One story I rather like is the one associated with the white lily.

One of the apostles, St Thomas, was not present at the death and entombment of the Blessed Virgin Mary and by the time he arrived the rock tomb in which her body was laid had been closed. Prevailed upon by his tears and entreaties, the other apostles opened the tomb; however, when they did so, they found that her body was gone and in its place lay a cluster of beautiful white lilies. Whatever the reason, the Madonna lily (*Lilium candidum*) has always been associated with the Virgin Mary. When they were no longer grown in the sacristan's garden, they continued to be grown in cottage gardens.

As well as flowers and greenery in church, the imagery of flowers, fruits and trees has been portrayed in stone carving, wood carving, stained glass and hangings. The craftsmen too used flowers and fruit as reminders of their significance.

With the passage of time one cannot state accurately what exact meaning any particular flower held; they may even have varied slightly from district to district and climate to climate. However, to the people who saw them, they meant something. Box, holly and ivy were symbols of the resurrection, cedars of the faithful, palms of victory, yew of death, and olive of peace. The white lily signified purity (indeed white flowers generally did, and still do, represent purity). The rose portrayed incorruption, while garlands of roses indicated heavenly joy. The vine represented 'Christ our life' and the grapes 'This is my blood'. Corn ears stood for the Eucharist.

The custom of bearing palm branches and willows on Palm Sunday, as a sign of victory, has of course continued down to the present day. Holly and ivy are still used at Christmas, the leaves of the holly, some say, representing the crown of thorns, and the red berries the blood shed by Christ on Calvary. Ivy denotes everlasting life. Lilies are widely used, especially on altars, as symbols of innocence, purity and joy. Cedar and yew are often incorporated in wreaths.

Tracing the usage of flowers in church, one can go right back to St Jerome (AD 346–420). In Hook's *The Church Dictionary* he quotes St Jerome who praises his friend Nepotian for using 'flowers of many kinds and the leaves of trees and branches of the vine in beautifying the church.'

At festivals all through the Middle Ages, and certainly up to the Reformation, garlands were placed before saints and on candlesticks. Clergy and choir carried garlands and even wore chaplets of flowers. As they processed into church, flowers were cast at them, which landed on the ground to join the sweet-smelling herbs already strewn there. The herbs signified purification for superstitious reasons, but doubtless served an added purpose at a time when the cleanliness of streets left a lot to be desired. Searching in archives, interesting items can be found like those recorded by Katharine McClinton:

Paid for rose garlands on Corp Xtie daye
A dozen and half rose garlondes on S Barnabus
Three dozen garlands for choir
For holly and ivy at Christmas
For byrch at Midsomer

Even as late as 1870 Kilvert in his diary (although perhaps not too seriously!) records:

> This evening being May Eve I ought to have put some birch and some wittan [mountain ash] over the door to keep out the 'old witch'. But I was too lazy to go out and get it. Let us hope the old witch will not come in during the night. The young witches are welcome.

The garlands referred to in the records were not necessarily always garlands as we think of them today in the shape of those delightful necklaces of flowers used in Hawaii and elsewhere. The garlands, for instance, carried by the clergy and choir were more probably flowers bunched and tied onto the end of a reed or light pole.

The saints too were remembered by their own flowers. An 'Old English Table of Flowers' is included at the back of this book, more for interest than for practical use. A modern version, shorter and differing somewhat, refers to:

Canterbury Bell	– St Augustine of England
Crocus	– St Valentine
Crown Imperial	– Edward the Confessor
Daisy	– St Margaret
Herb Christopher	– St Christopher
Lady's Smock	– The Virgin Mary
Rose	– Mary Magdalene
St Barnaby's Thistle	– St Barnabus
St John's Wort	– St John

Undoubtedly, many more festivals were kept, and the churches decorated for them, than is the case today. The Reformation of course was the principal factor responsible for this decline followed in the eighteenth century by the 'Age of Reason', a period of enlightenment when philosophy was the vogue and superstition had no place.

In 1845 the 'Harvest Festival' was introduced. This was in part a reintroduction of Lammas Day (1 August) and the earlier Anglo Saxon Hlafmaesse or loaf mass which went out with the Reformation, but because these were the bringing of 'the first fruits of our labours' in the shape of the first two leaven loaves baked from the new wheat, the harvest festival was an innovation as it was designed to take place at the end of harvest when 'all was safely gathered in'. Its purpose was that of thanksgiving to God for His goodness to us; the corn, fruit and flowers were there for a purpose.

Again referring to Kilvert's diary, 15 September 1871, there is a marvellous account of the decorating of a country parish church for the harvest festival.

... the school children were busy leasing out corn from a loose heap on the floor, sitting among the straw and tying up wheat, barley and oats in small sheaves and bundles ... The schoolmaster, the boys and I gathering stringed ivy from the trees in the castle clump. The Miss Baskervilles dressing the hoops for the seven windowsills with flowers and fruit ... Miss Sandell undertook to dress the reading desk, pulpit and clerk's desk and did them beautifully. Then Cooper came down with his men carrying magnificent ferns and plants and began to work in the chancel. One fine silver fern was put in the font. Gibbons undertook the font and dressed it very tastefully with moss and white asters under the sweeping fronds of the silver fern. Round the stem were twined the delicate light green sprays of white convolvulus. The pillars were wreathed and twined with wild hop vine falling in graceful careless festoons and curling tendrils from wreath and capital. St. Andrew crossed sheaves of all sorts of corn were placed against the walls between the windows, wheat, barley and oats with a spray of hopvine drooping in a festoon across the sheaf butts and a spray of red barberries between the sheaf heads. Bright flowers in pots clustered round the spring of the arches upon the capitals of the pillars, the flower pots veiled by a twist of hop vine. Mrs Partridge returned from Worcestershire this afternoon and brought two magnificent branches of real hops from the Worcestershire hop yards. These we hung drooping full length on either side of a text Mrs. V. had made, white letters on scarlet flannel, 'I am the Vine, Ye are the branches. Without Me ye can do nothing.' From the corners of this text Cooper hung two bunches of purple grapes. Two texts in corn on green baize, 'Praise ye the Lord' in wheat ears and 'Thanks be to God' in oats were placed over the doors inside. Outside the great door branches of apples and pears hung over the door. The gates were dressed with ferns, fruit and flowers. Following the outer arch, within a border of Spanish chestnuts, oak and acorn, elderberries, barberries and apples, was Mr. Evan's text in scarlet letters on a bright blue ground, 'Enter into His Gates with Thanksgiving.' An avenue of tall ferns and coleus led up the chancel. A row of the same plants stood along the alter steps, and dahlias were laid on brae fern along the altar rail bars. On either side of the entrance to the altar hung a splendid cluster of purple grapes, and along the rails were tied at intervals small sheaves of wheat and tall heads of Pampas grass. On the altar stood two sheaves of all corn with a paten between them worked in scarlet flannel bordered with corn and IHS worked in wheat ears. Above this hung a cross covered with scarlet flannel and adorned with corn barberries. On the windowsill above a larger sheaf of all corn in a moss field and upon the moss lay all fruit, plums, apples, pears.

It grew dark before we finished for the night. Some work had to be done by candlelight and much had to be left for to-morrow.

Forget about the style of the decorating which sounds typically Victorian with their incorrigible flare for over-decorating everything. What a happy picture it conjures up of men, women and children, from all sections of the community, working together in a common purpose. How interesting, too, to note the inclusion of the written word giving the message of the foliage and flowers.

In the United States at the beginning of this century, and in Britain after World War II, flower festivals became fashionable. That our beautiful churches are used in this way is a lovely and happy thing. Initially these festivals were really exhibitions of flower arrangements with the emphasis on the skill of the arranger. Soon the idea of having an overall theme evolved, thus providing added interest. I believe, however, that for many smaller parishes there lingers the fear that they are not skilled enough to stage a flower festival. There is no reason why people, whose only experience with flower arranging is putting a bunch of wallflowers in a jam jar, cannot be part of creating a flower festival that attracts hundreds of people and gives great pleasure. I know; we've done it! We can all give to the many people who come to our festivals not only the joy of the flowers themselves but a message and food for thought. The purpose of flowers in church must surely be, as it has always been, twofold.

For those who would like to adopt this approach, or perhaps already have, but have run out of ideas, the main part of this book is written. I will try to outline ideas for 'themes' that could be used.

The idea of thinking how best to raise money is, in my opinion, quite the wrong way of approaching most of the fund raising we, as church people, undertake. Surely if we aim for the enjoyment and fulfilment of everyone involved, both those on the organising side and the people who we hope will come to our event, then augmenting the funds will undoubtedly follow. We held a flower festival in our little country church during the weekend of the worst rioting in many of our cities. The gratitude we received from the many visitors who came was overwhelming. Time and again people said that despite the troubles in our country, here was a haven of peace and beauty; that coming to our festival had not only given pleasure to the eye and had stimulated thought, but had helped them regain perspective and hope for the future.

Often visitors ask about an individual flower, is it easy to grow and so on. They tell you about their gardens, and they enjoy a little chat. Others may tell you they came because their parents or grandparents were married in the church or are buried in the churchyard. They are pleased to be listened to and to be welcomed. Many people are interested in the theme and how it was researched, and may even add their own bits of information. We in turn have given them something to take away, both visually and thoughtfully.

Nowadays, when travelling is so costly, people are more

inclined to come as part of a day's or half-day's outing. For this reason I am sure it is a good idea whenever it is possible to have a second or even a third attraction. 'Teas,' especially if they can be in a pleasant garden near the church, are popular but, wherever it is served, tea is always welcome. Perhaps an exhibition of paintings, crafts or 'bygones' could be held, or a local flower or vegetable garden opened to the visitors.

For the most part it is the ladies who want to come to a flower festival and if there is something to interest the men as well, there is a better chance of not only getting people in the first place, but of making them happy too.

When people from a town or village, who are not, so to speak, 'regulars', come to a festival, it is very important to make them feel welcome and, who knows, they might be delighted to be asked to help another time.

The individuals who are involved in a festival may not all wish to arrange flowers; possibly they might be more interested in any research on the chosen theme. Alternatively, they might find their niche in helping with the second, third, or whatever attraction there is. By broadening the field there is more likelihood of being able to include men as well as women.

Obviously, the larger the cross-section of population that is involved, the greater the number of people they will bring, each from their own circle of friends and neighbours, to visit the festival and the other attractions.

Last, but certainly not least, do not allow the joy of the flowers themselves to begin and end in the church. Do make provision to ensure that as soon as the festival is over, as many arrangements as are not required to be left in the church are given to the sick and the elderly and to those who would enjoy them.

2 *The Planning*

I'll work on a new and original plan
(said I to myself – said I)

W. S. Gilbert

Let us assume that your church, chapel, or meeting has decided upon having a flower festival. The dates have been chosen and the hours during which it will be open agreed. They have determined the other attractions that are to be held in conjunction and have appointed people to organise them. Besides this, they have put someone in charge of advertising and another to organise the porch rota and, depending upon the size and scale of the festival, an organiser or a committee of two or three to plan the actual flower festival. There is no need to have a super flower arranger. What is wanted is someone with enthusiasm, imagination and the gift of getting the plan across.

THE ADVERTISING

Obviously this is all important, otherwise the whole effort is rather pointless! We all have our usual forms of advertising: posters, the parish magazine, etc. These, however, are not usually enough. Depending upon the size of the population you are appealing to, small handbills delivered with the newspapers are effective, provided they are simple and eye-catching. This may prove too costly. Alternatively, if every person involved with the festival has just a few to hand out to

friends who they think might be interested, this is excellent. I
say 'just a few' advisedly, because in my experience, if given a
pile to distribute, one gets put off and they just sit on the hall
table and finally end their days having their backs used for
shopping lists and telephone messages.

Local and provincial newspapers nearly all run a free
advertising service for 'What's on' any particular weekend. It
is surprising how many people that will bring. Your local radio
station probably provides a similar service. If you are
persuasive enough, your TV channel might do likewise. All are
very well worth trying.

THE PORCH ROTA

This involves the people allocated to be the hosts, as it were,
for the occasion. They are the ones whose job it is to make the
visitors welcome and to set the atmosphere on the day. It really
is best if you can have two people working together and, better
still, if at least one of them can answer questions about the
church, the flowers used, or any history or explanation on
queries regarding your theme.

We have a table in the church porch. On it we have a small
flower arrangement, our visitors' book, and a carboy. We
either sit behind the table or stand in the porch and as people
come in we welcome them, thank them for coming and invite
them to look around the church and ask if they will kindly sign
our visitors' book as they leave. This works well as it avoids
hold-ups in the porch. We have never asked for a donation.
People sign their names and drop one in the carboy.

If you have postcards or literature on sale, it would be best
to put these away from the porch. If you have an offertory box
for visitors in the church, I suggest you cover it up or do an
arrangement in it!

Sometimes a festival theme is chosen in the initial stages and
not left to the organisers. More often it is left to the planners
who can, of course, refer for approval after they have decided
upon it. The selection of a theme must, therefore, be the first
step.

CHOOSING THE THEME

The easiest way to begin is to make an assessment of your assets.

1 Availability of Decorators and Helpers
If this is your first festival, I am sure it is wise not to be too adventuresome and to go for something reasonably simple. Conversely, with a very imaginative group, you can be far bolder.

2 The Time of Year for Flowers and the Colours which Predominate
In the spring we are basically thinking of yellows and white. In the summer we have all colours and, of course, roses. Then come the autumn colours – bronzes, golds, berries and corn.

If you are buying flowers, particularly those which are imported, you have a wider range at any time. The amount of money, if any, allocated for buying flowers must also be taken into account.

3 The Style of your Church or Chapel
This is well worth thinking about. Some churches have vast, empty side aisles where you could lay out a border if you wished. Others are very dark, others majestic and bold, while some are simple and plain. Many have side chapels which, although within the main building, are quite separate and lend themselves to all manner of uses. Some churches have a cold and empty feeling, while others exude light and warmth. All these factors should be taken into consideration too when thinking about colour and design. For example, a large, lofty, cold-looking cream-washed building is not going to be greatly enhanced if decorated in yellow and white. It needs a mass of warmth of colour.

4 Any Outstanding Historical Features Connected with your Church or Town
It may be that an idea could present itself with this in mind. It

would certainly have popular appeal. Alternatively, if you can choose a theme which has a current significance or connection and you have an attractive title, it all helps to draw the crowds. We did 'A Festival of Wedding Flowers' the week before the wedding of the Prince and Princess of Wales. People were wedding-minded and we had a record number of visitors.

The main part of this book contains suggestions for themes; so, having made your assessment, we will assume that you have chosen a theme. Now I think it is wise to think about . . .

COLOURS

It is not, of course, essential to have a colour scheme. However, if there is no overall scheme of colour, you must be careful to see that there is some liaison, in a marriage of colour, between those arrangements in close proximity or viewed in the same line of vision. This is considerably more difficult in a small church; in which case, if you are not an experienced planner, it may well be easier to have a colour scheme.

If you are working to a colour range, I find the National Association of Flower Arrangement Societies circular chart in their *Guide to Colour Theory* most helpful. This is not expensive and available to non-members.

In a large church or cathedral you are probably able to work on a plan of four or five different colour schemes in various parts of the building which are separated from each other. If part A visually encroaches on part B then the colours can be married, as can B and C and so on.

Again, with colour one can make the best use of available assets. The sill beneath a stained-glass window or a heavy-looking dark pulpit may not appear to be assets, but of course they are, if used thoughtfully. If you have an arrangement which needs to be placed in front of a predominantly deep blue and deep red stained-glass window which has a touch of golden yellow or white on a halo or two, don't obviously use reds and blues because you will never see them and your arrangement will be lost. Use the gold or the white and bring out those colours in the windows so that each enhances the other. If you can find a light background near your window, you can of course complement the window by using similar colours. A sill beneath a window which is not stained glass and has a flood of light through it allows you to use heavier colours as they will be thrown up with the light behind them. Conversely, a dark pulpit front, for example, can make a lovely frame for white or pastel-coloured flowers.

Very often a pulpit, like a lectern, has a hanging which may well be matching an altar frontal. This should be borne in mind while selecting your colour scheme because you do not want the colours of the hangings to shout at your flowers or vice versa. A word of warning: do not assume that the colour of these hangings will be the same when you come to do the arrangements as they are when you plan them. Some churches may have only one set of hangings in permanent use, others may have several sets in different colours for use in the various seasons in the church's calendar. So do check. Recently I did the flowers for a wedding in a church with a beautiful oak altar. While I was in the church planning the flowers with the bride's mother, the verger came in and in passing remarked that he thought the altar frontal, which was away being mended and cleaned, would be back for the wedding. We checked up and, unfortunately, he was right.

Today the seasonal colours used for church hangings are basically:

Purple — Advent and Lent
Green — Sundays after Trinity and the Epiphany
Red   — Martyrs and Whit Sunday
White — Festivals of our Lord and all saints except martyrs

However, in the Sarum Rite, a well ordered colour sequence for use in the diocese of Salisbury from the eleventh century up to the Reformation, there were some fifty occasions for which the colour to be used was listed. A list is reproduced at the back of this book for those who may be interested. These colours have symbolic meanings which invariably vary very slightly depending upon one's source of information.

White   – The emblem of light, purity and innocence
Violet – Passion, suffering, penitence
Red   – Divine love, fire
Blue   – A serene conscience, truth, peace
Green – God's bounty, mirth, gladness, the resurrection

Although, of course, purple, green, red and white are still used as liturgical colours, it is possibly true to say that for many people it is perhaps only white and purple that hold any meaningful significance, perhaps because they alone are used traditionally beyond the liturgy.

Some churches have banners and tapestries, etc. Don't forget these. The carpets in the aisles, even in some cases the kneelers, can play a part.

Inevitably, in a hypothetical situation, the examples I have given are very obvious ones. Very often, however, it is the obvious that is missed. That extra thought behind each arrangement will give it that extra quality.

FLOWERS AND FOLIAGE

We have probably all been to a flower festival where magnificent arrangements were done with flowers obviously ordered *en bloc*. The net result was a collection of similar arrangements with the inevitable competitive undertone. The best way to create individuality, diversity and, therefore, interest, is for each arranger to pick or select her own flowers. If you have to buy flowers, there is no reason why a block order cannot then be given if you so wish. This obviously saves on carriage. If you are putting flowers down to expenses, then decorators must be given a cash limit.

The ideal is to have all garden flowers. People are usually very forthcoming in helping each other out. One person may have an abundance of silver foliage and not much else and another some super gladioli. By dint of giving to each other and getting bits and pieces from friends, it is quite possible to

Fig 1 Corn stalks, dried achillea, preserved copper beech and molucella are used with fresh flowers in this arrangement

manage without buying at all. How much nicer too, because you can use such a range of flowers and foliage. Apart from the result, in my opinion, being infinitely lovelier, it has added interest for the flower-minded gardener when visiting your festival.

The arrangement (Figure 1) is a happy mixture of fresh and preserved flowers and foliage. Corn, preserved copper beech, molucella (Bells of Ireland) and dried achillea have been used with fresh flowers and foliage.

I keep a nucleus of preserved flowers and foliage as can be seen by the reappearance of the molucella in the arrangement done almost a year later (Figure 34).

PLACING THE FLOWER ARRANGEMENTS

In many ways this, to me, is rather like planning a garden and I think this is a helpful approach. It is essential to have an overall plan so as to ensure that there is no overcrowding and indeed no dull gaps.

In a garden, however small, one does not really want to see it all at once. It is so exciting and lovely to turn a corner and find a beautiful vista ahead. Or, to come upon some treasure unexpectedly. When you walk up a garden path looking at a herbaceous border, it is equally lovely when you walk down. Nevertheless, there are plants you see on the way up that you can't see on the way down and vice versa.

This, of course, is the main difference in the planning of a flower festival as opposed to, say, decorating a church for a wedding. At a wedding the congregation is seated facing the altar. Thus, the main arrangements are viewed from the front only. In a festival this is not the case and this must be borne in mind in the planning. Because the visitors will be wandering about the church, looking, you have the advantage of having decorations in places that would never be seen if you were decorating for an actual service.

I am always amazed when I go to a new church to plan flowers for a wedding, how often the vicar, or whoever is taking me around, tells me where they normally have flower arrangements on these occasions and I find myself wondering 'why?' Invariably there is at least one arrangement that could not possibly be seen by more than three or four people once the pews are full of wedding guests either sitting or standing. With a flower festival this is not a problem and therefore gives you far greater scope.

When you move house and garden, you see possibilities that the previous owner had missed, because they had become complacent. So it is, I think, with our flower decorations in churches. A flower festival can be a golden opportunity for really having a good look around and asking, are we really making the best of our assets and potential?

When you make your plan, do it on a large sheet of cardboard. An old calendar backing is splendid, if you can find a big one, or the base of a large box. Make a floor plan of your building, scale doesn't matter, but indicate windows, doors, pillars, pulpit, altar, font and so on. Having chosen the placings for your arrangements, or groups of arrangements, number them as this is the easiest way to keep tabs on who is doing what. This is partly for your own use and partly because if arrangements 8, 9 and 10 are going to have to harmonise in colour, for example, then they know whom to contact. For the reference of all the helpers, it is a good idea to leave the plan, together with a corresponding numbered list with the decorators' names (addresses or telephone numbers are very helpful), along with a colour chart, in your vestry or church hall. These can then be accessible to all. The suggestion of having this list is purely for the facility of the helpers. Nothing could be further from my mind than the policy that was sometimes followed at early flower festivals of putting the decorator's name beside his or her arrangement.

Having made your plan, and before you have a get-together of all those involved, do consult your vicar, minister, priest, churchwarden or whoever the relevant person is, and obtain his approval. There is nothing more disappointing than having to take down or move an arrangement because there is some reason, of which you were unaware, whereby it should not be in that particular spot. It makes for harmony all round if everyone clearly understands what is going on.

When your list is complete seems a good time to point out to everyone that they are each responsible for clearing up any mess they make while decorating. This saves one person an awful lot of work! Also, to ask people to take great care to see that there is no damage to the church fabric, not only while decorating, but to use clear polythene or something similar under an arrangement if needs be. Many surfaces in an old church are uneven, which can cause spills and upsets. Have a good supply of plasticine in case anyone wants to get a container to stand level.

A diversity of form in your arrangements obviously greatly adds to the interest. As a planner you cannot always dictate terms on that score, but you can suggest, or even induce, what you want by means of imaginative placing of your arrangements. The suggestions in the following chapter may prompt you to a new idea.

3 The Places

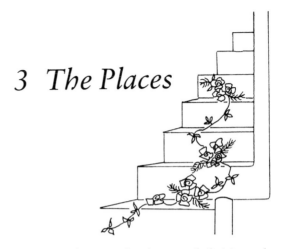

Proper words in proper places make the true definition of a style

Jonathan Swift

It would be an impossible task to cite all the places where arrangements could be positioned, every church or chapel being so individual. Instead, I shall give ideas úsed in one particular way, but which you could adapt to a similar use in quite another setting.

A little ingenuity and imagination will enable you to have an arrangement anywhere you choose.

STEPS

Steps, if you have them, are a gift: the possibilities endless. The simple arrangement (Figure 3) of roses and clematis, gently flowing down the rood-screen steps, is equally simple to do. This one is done using three saucers of similar colour to the steps, three oasis pegs, fix, and three cylinders of oasis (Figure 2).

There are, of course, pulpit steps, chancel steps, belfry steps and organ loft steps. You can create anything from a waterfall to gentle raindrops. Alternatively, you can think and arrange upwards! Your decoration can depict 'rising', 'ascending',

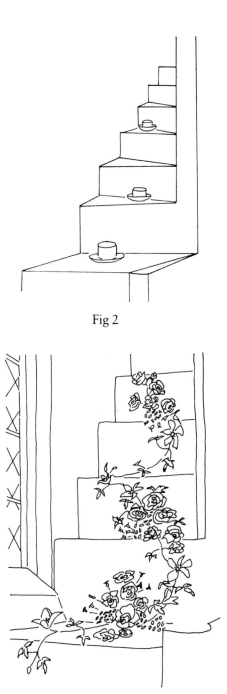

Fig 2

Fig 3 Roses and clematis gently flowing down rood screen steps, although simply contrived are visually very effective

'growing', 'climbing', and so on. Like the Roman Empire, you can rise and fall! Or perhaps just have a rock garden.

PILLARS AND POSTS

The sixteenth-century poet Edmund Spencer wrote:

'Youths now flock in everywhere
To gather May baskets and smelling briar
And home they hasten the posts to dight,
And all the church pillars ere daylight.'

Decorating pillars therefore is not a new idea; they certainly look very effective when decorated. It is sometimes easier to use fruits, foliage and dried material so as to avoid the complication of keeping flowers watered. The best method I know of attaching decorations is by using 'knicker' elastic spiralled down the post or pillar. The black metal post holding the paraffin lamp (Figure 5) has about 1.4m (1½yd) of black elastic wound around and down it, fixed securely top and bottom with the elastic kept fairly taut. Then, with finger and thumb, just lift the elastic sufficiently to poke the stem of your decorating material under it and then let it go back and it will hold things in place.

Fig 4

Fig 5 Hops, blackberries, hips and chinese lanterns decorate this delightful Victorian paraffin lamp by the method illustrated in Figure 4

You can either do your decorating as in Figure 5 or, in the case of a pillar, you might prefer to spiral it. Stylax lends itself well for this purpose but it is expensive and perhaps rather dull.

At harvest time you can use corn, in which case you won't need the elastic. With one person to hold the corn (ears uppermost), spread flat all round the post and with the ends cut off evenly, the second person can tie it in place with suitably coloured twine. Starting at the top, simply repeat the process in layers all the way down, each time just overlapping the cut ends. You can poke berries or dried flowers in here and there to liven it up. At Christmas time I do our posts with berried holly.

If you have either a groove or a band around your pillar at a suitable height, you can circle it with flowers. Use a circle of wire mesh and make one straight cut to the centre. Then place the wire mesh around the pillar. Using florist's wire join the cut edges together again, thus restoring your circle. With more florist's wire tie the netting securely around the pillar pulling the wire tight either in the groove or above the band. Cut suitably shaped pieces of well soaked oasis and place these around the pillar, at the same time bending the wire up and over to keep them in place.

You can hang garlands between pillars and posts and with suitably placed props, even create an archway or a pergola. An excellent idea, which is used for garlands, is to make a string of oasis sausages! Using plastic of similar thickness to that used for dustbin liners, machine long strips into 'sausage skins'. Then, using well soaked oasis in lieu of sausage meat, make as long a string as you require, tying firmly between each sausage and at either end. Poke holes in the plastic with a knitting needle so that you can get your flower stems into the oasis. An equally good alternative for the sausage 'skin' (and one that suits me better because my sewing machine is a 1930s' model) is to cut up green, plastic mesh sacks which I get from my greengrocer. Apart from obviously eliminating the necessity of having to make holes, the method of making your oasis sausages is exactly the same.

If you have neither a pillar nor a post, perhaps you have a churchwarden's staff that could do with embellishment.

CANDLE AND LAMP HOLDERS

Bracket candle and lamp holders are probably mostly to be found in rural churches where they make delightful receptacles for flower arrangements. Many are virtually disused, such as the lamp bracket on the organ (Figure 20). This type of bracket is remarkably adaptable as it is hinged and designed to be moved to give maximum light where needed. Thus one can move it to the most suitable position, in this case to enhance the gold pipes on this charming little organ. (The hymn book is open at the hymn 'I praised the earth, in beauty seen'.) Lamp or candle brackets on walls are ideal places for arrangements, especially as they are at a good height to be seen and enjoyed, and provide the perfect foil for a trailing or falling arrangement.

Altar candlesticks can double as flower vases too while still using them for their intended purpose, namely to symbolise Christ as the light of the world, ever present at the Holy Table. With the invention of electricity, we can have, at the flick of a switch, power, many hundreds of times that of one candle which inevitably results in the diminishing of the visual effect of the candles themselves. Using altar candlesticks for flowers as well as for their candles would certainly help to draw attention to them and act as a reminder of their significance for us.

The arrangement like the one in Figure 24, done for a wedding, could complement the bride's bouquet. I would not be without a pair of silver and a pair of gold-coloured candle cups in my flower cupboard (Figure 6).

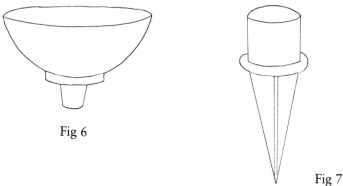

Fig 6

Fig 7

An oasis peg, some fix and a cylinder of oasis is all that is needed for each cup, with a green plastic candle holder (Figure 7) poked into the centre of the oasis.

Some churches have beautiful floor-standing candlesticks near the altar; these can easily be used for flowers. Candle cups and holders are too small in this case, so use something like a cake tin with a block of oasis held with a couple of oasis pegs. Remove the candle and make sure you protect the top of the candlestick before placing the tin onto it. Bend a piece of

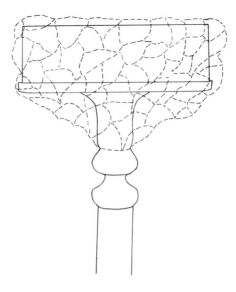

Fig 8

plastic-coated wire over the top of the oasis and round and under the tin, drawing it around the stem of the candlestick. Tie this in place and out of sight with string, rather than wire, so as not to damage the candlestick.

When replacing the candle, bear in mind that it is heavy and needs holding firmly. Find an empty, flat-bottomed, cylindrical plastic or tin container, the type used for detergents or polishes; the diameter of the container being sufficient to hold the candle without room for it to wobble. Cut off the top part of the container so that it remains just slightly taller than the depth of your oasis. Then, using the container like a biscuit cutter, simply push it through the centre of the oasis. Remove the oasis from within the container and place the container into the hole you have created in the oasis. Fix used on the base of this container should keep the candle steady. Slip the candle in when everything is tied up and secure. You will need to cut a small amount of your wire mesh, so be careful that any jagged ends are turned away so as not to damage the candle.

Wrought-iron candelabra are possibly better treated as 'pillars and posts' if their workmanship can be complemented rather than concealed.

The use of candlesticks and holders in relation to

interpreting your theme is obvious; used with candles you have 'light', or Figure 20 could be used as it is if you were doing 'Hymn Titles'. Whatever your theme, candle holders could fit into your plan beautifully.

WROUGHT-IRON GATES AND RAILS

Depending upon their design, these can be decorated using elastic and following the same method as that used for pillars and posts. If your wrought iron has scrollwork, you may be able to contrive small arrangements. Bear in mind that more than likely the finished product must look equally effective from both sides.

The vertical bars in the gates shown in Figure 35 have small sheaves or corn tied to them, in this case to form a cross. The sheaves have been tied with florist's wire below the ears, in the centre, and above the cut-off ends. So as not to damage the ironwork, black garden twine threaded behind the wire at the back of the sheaf was used to tie them to the gate. Obviously, you can place the sheaves in any design you like: arranged as lattice work is very effective. Having a decoration of this nature, which can be viewed from both sides, can be useful for illustrating some idea in your theme.

ROOD SCREENS AND ALTAR RAILS

Basically ideas for these are much the same as those in 'Wrought-iron Gates and Rails'. If, however, your screen is of delicately carved wood, it is probably advisable not to fix containers for fear of damaging the wood.

It may be that you have a rood loft, in which case you have ideal places for arrangements with perhaps lovely bits trailing down the verticals of the rood screen.

NOOKS AND CRANNIES

Under this heading come all those odd little places where, in the normal scheme of things, to have flowers would be a waste, as they might not be seen. Not so at a flower festival where they can prove the most delightful settings for the simplest vase of flowers and be so exciting to come upon. The little Gothic arch around the niche (Figure 28) makes a beautiful frame for a wine glass of 'Elizabeth of Glamis' roses.

Not all nooks or crannies are framed in such a way – some may be very narrow. A narrow niche can make the perfect place for a specimen flower, either in a vase or just lying. One perfect flower can be equally as effective as a big arrangement (Figure 24). If you have been fortunate enough to have been given an orchid, the container it comes in is ideal for keeping a single flower in water when it is laid flat. One flower can say a great deal and I think it is a lovely way of interpreting a thought or a meaning.

I use 'crannies' to cover the cut-out work in wood carving, for instance, a trefoil-shaped cut-out seems a fairly common decoration for the sides or front of a reading desk, prie-dieu, lectern, chairback, etc. Figure 9 shows such a trefoil. The depth of the wood, where it has been cut out, obviously varies. For a container use an empty plastic detergent bottle that fits very

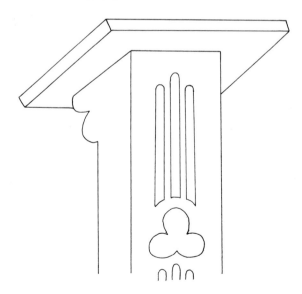

Fig 9

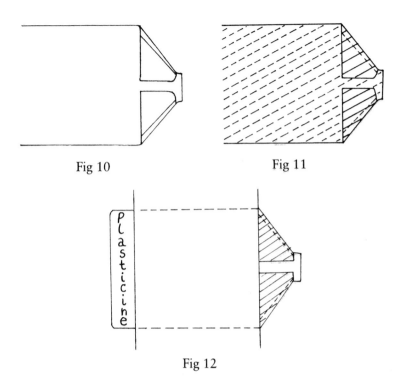

Fig 10

Fig 11

Plasticine

Fig 12

snugly into the top leaf of the trefoil. Remove and discard the cap and pourer and cut the top as Figure 10, leaving thin bands of plastic still affixed to the top and main body of the container. With this banded part of the container protruding beyond the face of the lectern, cut the bottom of the container off flush with the back of the lectern. Remove the empty container from the lectern and, using it like a biscuit cutter, fill it with oasis from a well-soaked block – the shaded part (Figure 11) now being oasis.

Replace the container within the lectern cut-out and block up the bottom of the container with plasticine that merges with the colour of the wood (Figure 12). This will stop any water escaping. If this can be put roughly in two halves, then the top half can be removed to add water if required. For a two-sided arrangement simply use two detergent bottles and telescope the cut-off ends.

I have set out in detail the method of making such a container because it is a useful one which can be used in a variety of places.

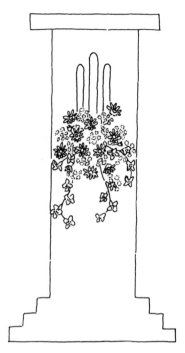

Fig 13 Ox-eye daisies, philadelphus stripped of its leaves and cow parsley arranged in a container as illustrated in Figures 10, 11 and 12

Any free-standing piece of furniture, the front of which can be seen as you go up the aisle and the back as you come down, makes an interesting position for a double-sided arrangement. For instance, if your theme was 'Hymn Titles', you could have 'The roseate hues of early dawn' on one side and 'As now the sun's declining rays' on the other. Perhaps in your theme you might wish to indicate two opposing thoughts, ideas or incidents.

An ornamental cabbage has been fixed into the reading desk cut-out on the back cover to complement those used in the harvest festival decorations elsewhere in the church.

Of course, there are other nooks and crannies, upon which it is not possible to generalise. I hope that you will have fun in finding them and fitting them into your scheme. It is so very often the subtle placing of an arrangement, however small, that can endorse the meaning of whatever you are trying to convey.

ARCHES AND ARCHWAYS

Unless an arch has been built in a convenient manner, it can prove a difficult place to affix a decoration. However, if you can manage it, you will be well rewarded.

Needless to say, a decoration over an arch, like decorations in wrought-ironwork and elsewhere, can easily be done with wired flowers. I have, however, avoided suggesting the use of wired flowers anywhere in this book because my personal feeling is that a flower festival is not the place for them. Again, therefore, we have to try to devise a method of securing some sort of container or containers so that the flowers and foliage can be in water. Plainly, if you use trailing foliage, such as clematis or ivy, you can cover a greater area and only one or two stems need to obtain water.

With this arch three very small round plastic lids are kept in place with a strong non-marking plasticine-like adhesive. The adhesive, put on so as to cause the container to tilt backwards towards the wall, will act as a counterbalance to the weight of the flowers and the foliage which protrude forwards. Fixing containers in old buildings is particularly difficult as you may find the plasterwork coming away with the adhesive, in which case you just have to abandon this method.

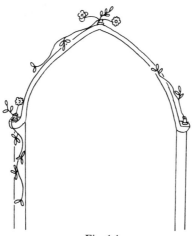

Fig 14

Fig 15

Alternatively, it may be possible to suspend a flower basket, or similar, from the ceiling.

You can then make a trailing decoration from your basket. It is not difficult to make your own basket using a disbanded metal coat hanger for the main frame and then to line it with meshed wire. This will then hold oasis foam. Making your own basket enables you to have one, or both, sides flat, which will help to keep it steady against the wall.

An arch, similar to the tiny one over the niche (Figure 28), with two small bundles of straw on it to look like thatch, looks very effective, with a nativity scene in the niche and a star on the peak of the roof, or suspended above it.

Not all arches, of course, prove difficult places to have containers and if you have a deep enough arch, where you can safely fix several containers around it, the finished decoration can be dramatic: a rainbow, for instance, with bands of violet, indigo, blue, green, yellow, orange and red; a sunset or a sunrise.

An arched way, rather than an arch, widens the scope for interpretation; not only an opening up, but a leading through; a looking forward and a looking back. Buds on one side, full blooms on the other indicating the lifespan. In the same vein, the cycle of the seed head to the full bloom and round again.

Once you have started making your plan and your mind is geared to that way of thinking, the solution as to the best use of a place, in conjunction with the interpretation of your theme, will present itself far more readily than thinking about it hypothetically, as one must do here.

WINDOWSILLS

There is nothing original about having floral arrangements on windowsills. They are probably the most popular of places. I think perhaps what is worth mentioning is what I have already touched on in the section on colour, namely the placing of the arrangement on the sill.

If your window is clear glass and your arrangement is placed centrally, then you have the light behind it and justice is not done to the flowers. If, however, the arrangement is placed on one side or the other, depending upon which angle you wish it to be viewed from, you then have the depth of wall behind it and the light on it. In the case of a window on a north wall, or where there is very little external light on to the window due to trees, buildings, etc, then it may be possible to have your arrangement placed centrally.

Not all windowsills are necessarily flat, many have a very precipitous slope down from the window. This, I think, is really an advantage rather than a disadvantage, because it enables you to show flowers off better and to create a diversity of shape in the form of arrangement. Containers can be built up so that they sit flat, parallel to the floor. However, as I have said, I think it is more effective to use the slope rather than to overcome it. The arrangement (Figure 34) done in this way

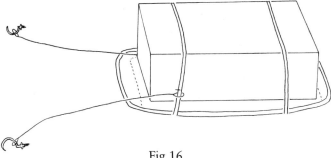

Fig 16

takes advantage of the slope so as not to have the light behind it, but on it, at the same time not obscuring the stained glass, but instead complementing it. The containers are small white trays, saved from a purchase of chicken pieces from the supermarket! A block of well soaked oasis was fixed on to each tray with two oasis pegs and some fix. Green flower tape was bound twice around the tray and the oasis in two places, a piece of florist's wire was then tied around each band of tape and the ends of the wires each fixed to a small cup hook. The hooks were then used, like grapnels, over the lead ledge at the base of the window (Figure 16).

More modern windows tend to have very narrow sills. The sill beneath the window (Figure 17) is only 5cm (2½in) deep. Here the base of a 50g (2oz) tobacco tin was used as a container and was quite adequate for the size of arrangement required.

Fig 17 The problem posed by a narrow sill in this modern chapel is overcome by using a small rectangular tin as a flower container

BITS AND PIECES

Baskets

In country churches the use of small baskets, or improvised containers, tied to the pew ends are a pretty touch (Figure 31). These baskets are lined with tin foil and hold oasis. A posy every two or three pews is really quite enough. It is quite possible to overdo it!

Stands

Using stands is very straightforward but make sure they are not placed in front of anything which might interfere with the background.

Single Flowers (used lying flat)

These can be kept in water by using something like an old plastic toothbrush container, with the open end sealed around the stem by packing with floral plasticine. The tube can then be bound with florist's tape. To avoid flattening the bloom raise the sealed end by placing a small piece of plasticine beneath.

A Bouquet of Flowers

The bride's bouquet (Figure 24) is an arrangement done in oasis kept in place with some fix and a peg in the lid of a rectangular 50g (2oz) tobacco tin. A 31.75cm (12½in) florist's wire, bent double, and bound with white wrapping ribbon finished in a bow, serves to give the effect of bound stems, when the two wire ends are inserted into the oasis.

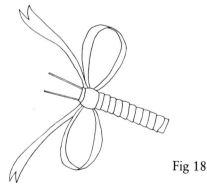

Fig 18

Pulpits
These may have a suitable side or front to create a good background for an arrangement.

The Rests
Reading desks and lecterns, etc, if not in use, are good places for arrangements. Any sort of flat container can be used and taped on to the sloping rest. You might want an arrangement shaped like a book or the container could be fixed with florist's tape at the top of the slope so that the flowers and foliage would hang down the opposite side as well (Figure 19) as was done for the arrangement on the back cover.

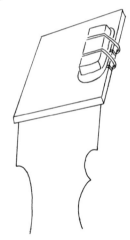

Fig 19

The Altar
It is right that mention should be made of the Holy Table, the focal point of any church. Whereas flowers and greenery were freely used in other parts of the church, the sanctioning of the usage of altar flowers was comparatively recent, although previously there had been flowers on the gradine. The question of the use of altar flowers evidently came before the Court of Arches and in 1870 they decided that 'the placing of vases of flowers on the Holy Table was an innocent and not unseemly decoration'.

There are many churches today where white flowers only are used on altars (and, of course, no flowers at all during

Lent). In 1914 Herbert Jones, who wrote from a country parish, published *Altar flowers and how to grow them*, in which book he speaks only of white flowers. In *British Floral Decoration* published in 1910 by R. F. Felton of London, he describes how for 'society weddings' he had 'been allowed a little latitude' with regard to using soft colourings on the altar. Certainly, when we are decorating for a flower festival, albeit not a festival in the church's calendar, the use of white flowers would give to the altar the special significance it holds for us as Christians.

These ideas for placings may help you not only to find new and interesting positions for your arrangements, but also to endorse the meaning of what you are trying to convey with your flowers. A thought or idea will frequently determine its own placing.

So now to the 'Themes'.

'There is nothing new under the sun.' An old adage that proves itself, all too often, very true when one is trying to think of an original idea, in this case the choice of a theme or title for a flower festival. What can be original is the interpretation of that theme. By that I do not mean the excellence of the actual flower arrangements, but rather what I have tried to convey in this and the previous chapters, namely the emphasis that can be given to conveying a point by, one could almost say, the hints, given by its thoughtful placing, colouring or shape. Therefore, if a particular theme has been used previously in other churches, but your assessment of your assets points to it being a good one for you, go ahead and do it.

It is not possible to say of any particular theme that it is a good or a bad one for beginners. The success of anything is achieved by the amount of thought and work put into it. Someone organising her first flower festival may well have infinitely more imagination than a so-called expert and be a wizard at conveying her ideas and enthusiasm to others.

There is, therefore, no significance attached to the order in which the following suggestions are written. I hope, rather, that they will help you to arrive at a choice of theme, even possibly one that is not mentioned here.

 # 4
Hymns

I praised the earth in beauty seen
With garlands gay of various green

Bishop Heber

I have no doubt that this theme has been used many many times, but of course there are a great many hymns to choose from and it is by no means necessary to stick always to the first line or the first verse. There are plenty of equally suitable lines and verses. I think if people choose their own hymns it is bound to work better, because they will undoubtedly have in conjunction with their selection an idea for interpreting them. Of course, if they want help, then you must have a few ideas up your sleeve.

The first festival we did was 'Hymns' and all us womenfolk did an arrangement. One dear lady made no bones about the fact that she had no idea how to arrange flowers, but I'm glad to say that she was very keen to help and declared she wanted to do 'All things bright and beautiful'. I admit I was rather apprehensive as to what the result might be, but I need not have worried. She had the most lovely copper jug which she polished until it really shone. In it she put three truly perfect roses. Although she had insisted on a rather out-of-the-way place for her arrangement, it was very much admired and enjoyed.

If you provide the white cardboard, or whatever you plan to have the verses written on, school teachers of the senior schools are usually very helpful in getting pupils to write them in script for you. I think white card with black script writing is easy to the eye.

Looking through your hymn book, it won't take you long to find something that appeals to you. For example, T. Ellerton's 'This is the day of light, let there be light to-day' is a good one to be the first seen inside the church. Or another of his, 'Our day of praise is done, the evening shadows fall' would be appropriately placed so that it is seen as you leave, but not as you come in. Part of the second verse of the old hymn which begins 'Now wonders of Thy mighty hand' – 'The sun is ruler of the day, the silver moon by night' is lovely if you have a place where you can do a two-sided arrangement. The colours here, as in all the hymns, speak for themselves. Some other suggestions: from verse 5 of Mrs Alexander's well known hymn 'The ripe fruits in the garden, – He made them every one'; Bishop Mant's 'Bright the vision that delighted'; the hymn by N. Tate and N. Brady, 'Through all the changing scenes of life' – perhaps seed heads to full blooms round an arch, or perhaps a colour range; another of Mrs Alexander's hymns, 'There is a green hill far away'; J. Hampden Gurney's 'Fair waved the golden corn'; the hymn by E. H. Plumptre, 'O light whose beams illumine all, from twilight dawn to perfect day' – What a blueprint for colour!

You may find it interesting to delve into the history of hymns. When and why were they written? Like poetry, hymns were often inspired by an event or written to commemorate some occasion. I always enjoy a hymn much more when the vicar says that it was written by such a one on such an occasion, and explains a bit about it, thus making the words more meaningful. For example, the lovely hymn by Dean Alford (1810–71)

> Come ye thankful people, come,
> Raise the song of Harvest-home:
> All is safely gather'd in,
> Ere the winter storms begin;
> God, our Maker, doth provide
> For our wants to be supplied;
> Come to God's own Temple, come;
> Raise the song of Harvest-home.

is interesting from the historical point of view. The harvest festival, as we know it, was probably first introduced in 1845 by Dr Hawker, and was largely conceived to counteract the wild goings on at the harvest horkeys (harvest suppers), which

were the cause of much concern to the clergy. How subtly
Dean Alford cajoles his people, celebrating the finish of
harvest, into putting the emphasis of celebration where it
belongs.

J. H. Newman, later Cardinal Newman, wrote his hymn
'Lead, kindly Light, amid the encircling gloom' after a time of
personal conflict in his faith following his involvement with
the Oxford Movement and his subsequent decision to leave
the Anglican Church and join the Church of Rome. The 'angel
faces' he refers to in the last verse indicate his friends in the
Anglican Communion from whom, in life, he was now
separated, but with whom he would be reunited after death.
The thinking by Newman and others at this time represented a
striking landmark in the varied notions of English religious
thought.

You may think that a leaflet with one or two brief
explanations on some of your hymns might encourage the
visitor to read the verses more thoughtfully. Your vicar would
be able to help you find suitable information. I feel sure it is an
idea well worth exploring.

Lastly, you may think that these two verses are lovely ones
to use at your festival whether you are having hymns or not
from the hymn by A. G. W. Blunt:

Verse 1

Here, Lord, we offer Thee all that is fairest,
Flowers in their freshness from garden and field;
Gifts for the stricken ones – knowing Thou carest
More for the love than the wealth that we yield.

Verse 4

We, Lord, like flowers in our Autumn must wither;
We, like these blossoms, must fade and must die:
Gather us, Lord, to Thy bosom for ever,
Grant us a place in Thy home in the sky.

Verse 1, to be read as people go into the church, sets the tone; verse 4 to read as they leave and to take away in their minds. Surely these two verses say a great deal.

Fig 20 The lamp bracket on this seventeenth-century organ makes a charming receptacle for a posy of roses, chrysanthemums, nicotiana and hips

5
Poetry with Flowers

Make poetry and give pleasure

Horace

This is a lovely one to do. Not many people actually sit down and read their favourite poems in the same way as they might put on their favourite records or cassettes. Nevertheless, they enjoy reading them when they see them again.

I have titled this 'Poetry with Flowers' deliberately, because the flowers must express exactly what the poem is saying, one cannot alter the meaning to suit one's convenience! On the face of it this may seem to you a rather difficult theme, but I don't really think so. By no means am I suggesting that you choose poems literally about flowers. The following lines, and I regret that, so far as I am concerned, the author is unknown, may help to show what I mean.

> Whatever the time, the hour or the place,
> Or the trouble and toil there may be in the case –
> I verily think, that we never can measure
> The pleasure there is, in the giving of pleasure.

These lines together with flowers arranged in a basket, as you might give to someone in hospital, is a very simple and attractive thought. As I see it, there is very little point in using verses which do not have some sort of helpful thought or message or provide food for thought and enjoyment. Apart from anything else, your success rate of giving pleasure must surely be doubled: the pleasure of both mind and eye.

We all have our favourite poems and doubtless everyone would come up with their own. Equally, it is helpful to have a few examples to stimulate ideas.

For an autumn festival a few lines from Keats' 'To Autumn' would be lovely:

Season of mists and mellow fruitfulness
Close bosom friend of the maturing sun;
Conspiring with him how to load and bless
With fruit the vines that round the thatch eaves run.

A great favourite of mine is the first verse of Minnie Louisa Haskin's poem:

I said to the man
who stood at the gate of the year,
'Give me a light that I may tread safely into
the unknown.' And he replied, 'Go out into
the darkness and put your hand into the
hand of God. That shall be to you better
than light and safer than a known way.'
So I went forth and finding the hand of God,
trod safely into the night. And he led me
towards the hills and the breaking of day
in the lone East.

Flowers in the colours of the breaking day arranged by an east window could be most effective. You might think of another interpretation.

For a suitably situated archway, these lines from Tennyson's *Ulysses* could be illustrated:

I am a part of all that I have met
Yet all experience is an arch wherethro'
Gleams that untravell'd world, whose margin fades
For ever and for ever when I move.

Four lines taken from William Blake's *Auguries of Innocence*,

> To see the world in a grain of sand
> And a Heaven in a wild flower
> Hold infinity in the palm of your hand
> And eternity in an hour

together with an arrangement of wild flowers, would be beautiful anywhere.

There are many poems about spring, if you are having your festival in springtime. Perhaps A. A. Milne's 'Daffodowndilly' might appeal to the young visitor:

> She wore her yellow sun-bonnet,
> She wore her greenest gown;
> She turned to the south wind
> And curtsied up and down.
> She turned to the sunlight
> And shook her yellow head,
> And whispered to her neighbour:
> 'Winter is dead.'

In Chapter 3 I have suggested using somewhere like a lectern for a double-sided arrangement and cited arrangements of two opposing subjects. Were you to use the lines from Shakespeare's *Hamlet*, Act I, Scene 3,

> This above all: to thine own self be true,
> And it must follow, as the night the day,
> Thou canst not then be false to any man.

you could portray them with two absolutely identical arrangements on the two faces of the lectern.

Part of the charming poem called 'Ducks', written by F. W. Harvey while in a prison camp in World War I, calls for an arrangement of little flowers, including, of course, daisies.

> When God had finished the stars and whirl of coloured suns
> He turned His mind from big things to fashion little ones,
> Beautiful tiny things (like daisies) He made, and then

He made the comical ones in case the minds of men
   Should stiffen and become
   Dull, humourless and glum,
And so forgetful of their Maker be
As to take even themselves – quite seriously.

How about a verse from 'Sherwood' by Alfred Noyes:

Merry, merry England has kissed the lips of June
All the wings of fairyland were here beneath the moon
Like a flight of rose-leaves fluttering in a mist
of opal and ruby and pearl and amethyst.

Then, too, there is the poetry of the Bible, the song of Solomon, many many other beautiful passages and the psalms.

The earth is the Lord's,
and all therein is:
the compass of the world,
and they dwell therein.

                   Psalm 24, verse 1

Then shall the earth bring forth her increase:
and God, even our own God,
shall give us his blessing.

                   Psalm 67, verse 6

Also from the Bible, St Paul's first epistle to the Corinthians, Chapter 13 and starting at verse 1, that lovely passage beginning

Though I speak with the tongues of men
and of angels
and have not charity
I am become as a sounding brass
or a tinkling cymbal.

Lastly, there is no reason why verses of hymns should not be used. Perhaps C. A. Allington's hymn

Lord of beauty, thine the splendour
Shewn in earth and sky and sea,
Burning sun and moonlight tender,
Hill and river, flower and tree:
Lest we fail our praise to render
Touch our eyes that they may see.

serves to remind us of what it is all about.

Do try to have the poems written in sufficiently large writing so that people can read them easily. Again, black script writing on white card is very effective and equally attractive. In order to cement yet soften the tie between the flowers and the words, some form of floral cartouche to the written word is a most attractive addition.

Should you have an artist in your community, then the cartouche could be painted. Pressed or dried flowers might be used; suggestions for this method are set out in Chapter 18. Alternatively, you can use fresh flowers either by garlanding your flowers (Figure 25, page 57) in whatever shape is best suited to the words, oval, rectangular, etc, or by simply affixing a posy of flowers, or just one flower, if that seemed more appropriate. I find an excellent idea for posy containers is to get empty plastic syringe cases from your vet! These are made of clear plastic and about 11cm (4½in) long. Cut a semi-circle out of the neck of the container, which enables you to 'arrange' the flowers rather than having to 'jam' them in. The cut-out semi-circle would be the front, ie the side from which the flowers would be seen. Having arranged the flowers, lay the container on its back on the card, at an angle so that the water will not spill, and fix it in position with sellotape. Before fixing the container of flowers, mark out and cut two slits either side of the container stem in order to thread a ribbon from the back of the card. The ribbon can then be tied in a bow to conceal the flower stems and the container (Figures 21 and 22).

To have one flower only, simply use the method suggested for a single flower, page 41. This can either be fixed by the same method as the posy or, if the back of your card will not be visible to the visitors, simply make a suitably sized hole in your

Fig 21   Fig 22

card and poke the container through it from the front (Figure 23). With a garland or posy, using small varieties of the flowers used in your main arrangement, and in similar colouring, is particularly attractive.

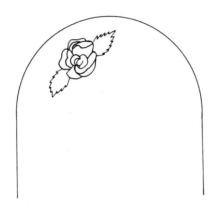

Fig 23

There are many ways of decorating your words, indeed the words themselves may prompt an idea. Rather than propping your decorated writings up against something, they look much better if they are free standing. This is easily done by glueing a wedge-shaped cardboard leg support firmly on to the centre back of your 'picture'; fixed, so that the picture tilts backwards slightly. This is best done after the writing is complete and before the flowers are added, unless, of course, the cartouche is painted or done in pressed flowers, in which case that would need to be done first while the picture could still be laid flat.

6
Wedding Flowers

With flowers the bridal path bestrew

Anon.

I think this theme is possibly one which lends itself better to a small church. The idea is simply to imagine that there is to be a wedding. The only decisions, therefore, are what colourings the bride and bridesmaids will wear and how many of the latter there are to be. Not, of course, that any of them will be there! They will be portrayed by their bouquets and the colourings of these will determine the harmonising colours for the decorations in the church.

I am often amused when I am asked to do wedding flowers to see whether it is mum or daughter who has the final say in the matter! The worst situation is the one that arises when both are quite determined that they are going to leave it to you and equally determined that whatever they choose in the way of colours for dresses has no bearing on the matter; so you simply choose your own collection of colours and hope for the best!

With a festival, of course, you have the advantage of choosing colouring that will suit your church and is readily available from the garden at the time of year you are considering. If you work on that basis, then even if you have several 'mums' on your committee you will probably all agree!

Choosing the colouring to suit your church in conjunction with the time of year is not the only advantage you gain over the 'live' situation. You have the added advantage of being able to have arrangements in places you would not consider if you had a church full of people in the pews. Having said that, if of course you start filling the pews up with flowers, you will detract from the imaginary situation of people present. I refer rather to the fact that it is not necessary to place arrangements in such a way as they may be seen by a congregation, but on this occasion by the visitor who will be looking both up and down the church, and who is not rooted to his seat in a pew.

My personal preference at weddings is that the altar flowers should be white, bearing in mind that this is not always possible if you have a light-coloured backcloth. Beyond this, the placing is aesthetic and is not complicated by the significance of its positioning. The flower that is by tradition associated with weddings is the sweet-smelling white orange blossom. In symbolism orange blossoms signified virginity, and the custom of their use for wedding decorations was introduced into England, from France, about 1820. The orange is said to indicate the hope of fruitfulness (few trees are less prolific) and the white blossoms to symbolise innocence. We do not, of course, grow oranges in this country but we have the 'mock orange' philadelphus (which some of us, apparently incorrectly, formally knew as syringa!). The single or the double variety is equally lovely and if you can bring yourself to remove all the leaves, then an arrangement of philadelphus against a dark background is particularly beautiful. It is easily obtained from gardens in June and into July.

Having set the stage, all that remains, therefore, is the actors: the bride and groom, the bridesmaids, and the best man too if you like! The bride and groom make their vows at the chancel steps. A white bouquet and a white buttonhole laid on the steps look well as substitutes (Figure 24). Details of how to arrange these can be found under 'Bits and Pieces', page 41.

Then there must be some bridesmaids. Two tiny baskets of flowers on the floor would indicate the younger ones and further back perhaps two older bridesmaids. One idea for bridesmaids' posies is given under 'Pillars and Posts', page 28; alternatively they could be attached to a pew end. Attractive little Victorian posies are easily made. You can buy from a florist specially designed, cone-shaped, white plastic holders. Where you would expect to find a dollop of ice-cream, you find a cleverly secured dollop of oasis! To set the flowers off, a circular, plastic, doily-like frill fits round the neck of the cone. I find these frills enhanced by the addition of lace or suitable material stuck onto them.

The word posy is a contraction of the word poesy, meaning a verse or sentence inscribed possibly on a ring. The meaning of posy as a bunch of flowers, or nosegay, probably comes from the custom of sending verses with gifts of flowers which, in a sense, is what we are trying to do. You may care to use verses from hymns such as 'How welcome was the call' by Sir H. W. Baker:

> O Lord of life and love,
> Come Thou again to-day;
> And bring a blessing from above
> That ne'er shall pass away.

or Mrs Gurney's

Fig 24 White roses, carnations and gypsophila judiciously arranged in a small, flat container to which a wired bow has been added (Figure 18) create this bride's bouquet; the single rose alongside represents the bridegroom

O perfect Love, all human thought transcending,
Lowly we kneel in prayer before Thy Throne,
That theirs may be the love which knows no ending,
Whom Thou for evermore dost join in one.

Alternatively, you may choose suitable verses from elsewhere
or reproduce extracts from the marriage service.

An attractive idea is to contrive your written words onto a
card cut in a circular shape; it can then be 'ringed' with a
garland of flowers emulating the colour and flowers you are
using for your arrangements (Figure 30). To fix a garland
around writing in this way you would need, in addition to the
circular card with the writing, a second circle approximately
15cm (6in) larger in diameter, ie 7.5cm (3in) all round. This
bigger circle needs to be made of something more substantial
than cardboard. Plywood is ideal, perhaps you could get off-
cuts, or it might be cheaper to get a whole sheet (it would not
matter if it were marked or slightly damaged), and get as many
circles and leg supports as you require cut from it. Attach the
oasis sausage around the edge of your plywood circle by
stapling across the sausage skin where it is tied, rather than
through it. (I borrow a heavy stapling machine from the local
shop.) Next, glue firmly four empty cotton reels, or something
similar, at 12, 3, 6 and 9 o'clock of your plywood circle. Glue
the free ends of your cotton reels and stick the back of the
smaller cardboard circle (indicated by the dotted lines in

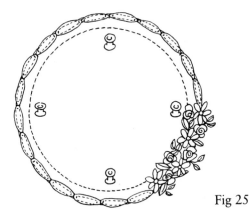

Fig 25

The Parishioners of Hoo
request the pleasure
of your company
at

'A Festival of Wedding Flowers'

in St Andrew's Church, Hoo
on Saturday July 11th
and Sunday July 12th 1982
from 2.00 - 6.30 p.m.

Teas in garden next door

Fig 26

Figure 25) with the writing already on the front of it, onto them. The writing, standing clear as it now does of the oasis sausage, will not be in danger of being dripped upon and smudged. All is now ready to arrange your flowers and leaves.

The leg support would have been affixed to the back of the plywood circle initially. Cutting these circles and fixing their leg supports is a splendid job for the men. Do, however, assure them that their creations will be saved to be used on future occasions.

When we had a festival of wedding flowers in our little church, we advertised it by means of small handbills (kindly distributed by the paper lady), which took the form of a wedding invitation (Figure 26). Posters could be done in the same way and, being an attractive and novel form of publicity, would certainly attract attention.

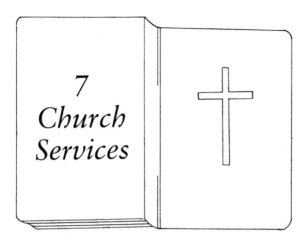

7
Church Services

O Worship the Lord in the beauty of holiness

J. S. B. Mansell

To portray the service of Holy Communion, Morning Prayer, Evening Prayer, Baptism and the Marriage Service would be enough in a small church. The area given to one particular service would obviously depend upon the size of the church. If room permitted, one could have a sample from each service, colourwise, to greet you going in and coming out.

The placing of the five services within the church is straightforward. Holy Communion would be in the sanctuary. On the assumption that the church is built with the altar at the east end, I would have the Morning Service on the south side of the church with the sun, and the Evening Service on the north side without the sun. How much of each side is given over to each service is entirely dependent upon the layout of the church. The font will undoubtedly be at the back of the church, so that area can be designated to Baptism. The bride and groom, if they were there, would make their marriage vows at the chancel steps. So the Marriage Service occupies the chancel.

I think a very brief explanatory leaflet would help the

visitor, if for no other reason than to ensure that the services are viewed in the designed order. Probably the service of Baptism first, followed by Morning Prayer, then the Marriage Service, the service of Holy Communion and finally the Evening Service. The latter viewed as the visitor comes back down the nave means that the blessing at the end of the Evening Service completes the tour, so to speak. If this is not practical, then have the blessing in the porch to be seen on leaving rather than arriving. There is no reason why you cannot have a little prayer on your leaflet too, and why not encourage visitors not to feel hurried, but, if they so wish, to sit in the pews and enjoy the peace and beauty.

THE SERVICE OF BAPTISM

The font is obviously the focal point and needs an eye-catching decoration around its base. Pink for girls, blue for boys and white for innocence and purity. Figure 29 using white daisies to depict innocence and ivy to indicate everlasting life, shows how an unusual font can be decorated. Both here and in the whole area surrounding the font delicate arrangements are called for. In small churches this area is limited. In large churches there is room for many arrangements.

I think the strength of the written word, to portray the service of Baptism, possibly lies in its brevity. Probably four extracts from the service would suffice. For example,

Suffer the little children to come unto me and forbid them not; for of such is the Kingdom of God.

Wilt thou be baptised in this faith?

Wilt thou then obediently keep God's holy will and commandments and walk in the same all the days of thy life?

I will.

Each extract could be garlanded in white daisies symbolic of purity and innocence and written on pale blue or pale pink card depending upon its proximity to a blue and white or pink and white arrangement.

MORNING PRAYER

The flowers here would be lovely in the brighter colours of the morning, the number of arrangements again depending on availability of space. Upon this too would depend the amount of the service that could be portrayed. The idea is to run through the service as it is set out. Whether you take the form of service from the Book of Common Prayer or the Alternative Service Book is the choice of each individual church. In either case the service starts with a sentence or introduction. Part of this one taken from the Alternative Service Book seems appropriate:

> We have come together as the family of God
> in our Father's presence to offer him praise
> and thanksgiving, to hear and receive his
> holy word, to bring before him the needs of the
> world, to ask his forgiveness for our sins and
> to seek his grace, that through his
> Son Jesus Christ
> we may give ourselves to his service.

There then follows the general confession followed by the absolution or pardon. Were you to use the above sentence, then perhaps you could omit the confession and go on, again in the Alternative Service Book to part of the pardon:

> Almighty God, who forgives all who truly
> repent, have mercy upon you, pardon and
> deliver you from all your sins.

Then comes the Venite or the Jubilate. How about a couple of lines from the latter:

> Come into his gates with thanksgiving and into
> his courts with praise:
> Give thanks unto him and bless his holy name.

Following this comes a psalm. Again I see no reason to use the first couple of lines if you find others you think more meaningful for your purpose. The last verse of Psalm 23, for example, might be a good follow-on:

> . . . thy loving-kindness and mercy shall follow me
> all the days of my life and I will dwell in the
> house of the Lord for ever.

Then comes the first lesson. Obviously one would think to have this arrangement on the lectern, however, as you have the Evening Service to consider, and also as it would probably mean infiltrating the area designated for the Marriage Service, perhaps you could find portable lecterns to use for Morning and Evening Services.

The passage chosen can be short and easily remembered. How about Genesis, Chapter 28, verse 16:

> Surely the Lord is in this place; and I knew
> it not.

Next the Te Deum, or you may again prefer the Jubilate,

> Serve the Lord with gladness,

what better title could you have for a lovely arrangement in the colours of the morning. Then comes the second lesson, this time from the New Testament, St John, Chapter 14, verse 6:

> I am the way, the truth, and the life, no man
> cometh unto the Father, but by me.

The first line of the creed, which is said next, is another lovely accompaniment to an arrangement,

> I believe in God the Father almighty,
> maker of heaven and earth.

Next comes the Lord's prayer. As this is said at all the services, it could effectively be divided into five and a sentence said at each service. This is followed by the prayers. You might choose to have a prayer suitable to your church's need or perhaps one from the Alternative Service Book, which would seem appropriate to end Morning Prayer with,

Eternal God and Father, you create us by
your power and redeem us by your love: guide
and strengthen us by your Spirit, that we may give
ourselves in love and service to one another and
to you: Through Christ our Lord. Amen.

You can put in as many hymns as you wish to accommodate.

The collages, whether painted, or done with fresh or dried flowers, again in the bright colours of the morning, would look sunny on yellow paper and perhaps you could have a butterfly or a bee depicted here and there to add to the atmosphere.

THE MARRIAGE SERVICE

Rather than repeat myself, the layout here could be very much as that given for 'Wedding Flowers', Chapter 6. For the colouring in the chancel and possibly including the choir stalls, perhaps yellow and white or cream and pink depending upon your surroundings. The card used could be cream. I think it is a good idea with this theme to change the colour of the card for each service as well as the flower colouring and then it makes it quite clear which belongs to which. Tiny half-circle garlands, like headdresses, would be attractive, either over or under the writing. The written word here, like that for the Baptism Service, I think should be limited to three or four different extracts. Not all necessarily from the Wedding Service, perhaps one or two hymns or a prayer,

. . . the Lord mercifully with his favour
look upon you; and so fill you with all
spiritual benediction and grace, that ye may
so live together in this life, that in the world
to come ye may have everlasting life.

THE COMMUNION SERVICE

Because of its placing in the sanctuary, and its significance amongst the sacraments, I feel that the flowers should be white if possible. The joy and purity of white is obviously most meaningful. If you like, white could then be introduced into all the other services together with their own colours.

The bread and the wine are the central part of the Communion Service. It may be that your church has a proper place in the sanctuary where the cruets and the bread are kept. Alternatively, they can be indicated by other means. The way that appeals to me the most is effective in its simplicity, like the altar arrangement (Figure 33) where a bunch of red grapes is hung out of a chalice or stemmed wine glass, perhaps with a vine leaf to hide the stem of the bunch of grapes, and a small loaf of white bread nearby. Correctly, of course, when having grapes one should have wheat ears, and having bread one should have wine; whether wheat ears or bread is up to you.

The sanctity of the Communion Service is possibly better portrayed without too much of the written word, especially as it probably will not be a case of walking from one arrangement to another, but rather of seeing them all at once. Any suggestions I give, for any of these services, are obviously only to give you the idea. What wording you use is the choice of each individual church. For Holy Communion I would suggest:

Come unto me all that travail and are heavy
laden and I will refresh you.

Were this written on a white card, then instead of emulating the white flowers, which would not show up against it, perhaps red (wine)-coloured flowers could be used to decorate the card.

EVENING PRAYER

The same 'system' would apply to the Evening Service as applied to the Morning Service. The colouring would differ and I would suggest the pink to violet hues of the sunset with the wording on pale greyish-violet card with the collage matching the flower colouring. It is important not to have the cardboard, in any instance, in too dark a shade otherwise the lettering will not stand out sufficiently. The stage could be further set with a smattering of hymn books on the pews, open at evening hymns, and prayer books open at Evening Prayer.

The opening sentence for Evening Prayer in the Alternative Service Book being the same as that for Morning Prayer, perhaps one from the Book of Common Prayer would be better here, first book of St John, Chapter 1, verses 8 and 9,

If we say that we have no sin, we deceive
ourselves, and the truth is not in us; but if
we confess our sins, he is faithful and just to
forgive us our sins, and to cleanse us from all
unrighteousness.

Then the confession and the pardon. Again you may find it best to omit one or both or to have both and omit the psalm or, space permitting, have the lot!

Then follows the Old Testament lesson, again, something short and to the point would seem wise – Ecclesiastes, Chapter 6, verse 16:

A faithful friend is the medicine of life.

The Magnificat comes next, and to hope for a statue of the Virgin Mary, conveniently at the stage, would be asking a great deal. There are, however, Madonna lilies, and as they are so meaningful in themselves, perhaps the statue would be superfluous anyway.

Then comes the New Testament lesson, St John, Chapter 15, verse 16:

Ye have not chosen me, but I have chosen you.

and this is followed by the Nunc Dimittis, particularly lovely when accompanied by the evening colours. The Nunc Dimittis is followed by the creed, which you may choose to omit here, having used it in the morning service, or indeed you may elect to give it added strength by using it twice. Then the service turns to the prayers, perhaps the collect,

> Lighten our darkness, we beseech thee, O Lord;
> and by thy great mercy defend us from all perils
> and dangers of this night; for the love of thy
> only Son, our Saviour, Jesus Christ. Amen.

Finally, comes the blessing. You may instead, or indeed as well, elect to use the prayer of dedication from the Alternative Service Book.

> Almighty God,
> we thank you for the gift of your
>   holy word.
> May it be a lantern to our feet,
> a light to our paths,
> and a strength to our lives.
> Take us and use us
> to love and serve all men
> in the power of the Holy Spirit
> and in the name of your Son,
> Jesus Christ our Lord. Amen.

If your church has side chapels, then you can incorporate the festivals as well. Easter, Whitsun, Christmas and so on, (Chapter 16).

Should you have an area of marble memorials and effigies of people, I see nothing wrong with remembering them with a wreath apiece. You can buy circular plastic containers tightly filled with oasis which are suitable for wreaths. These, when complete, can be placed at any angle you choose. As to colours, I am sure these people might have family crests and some research into their colouring might be interesting. Alternatively, you could use the whole range of purples, from pale lilac to deep purple.

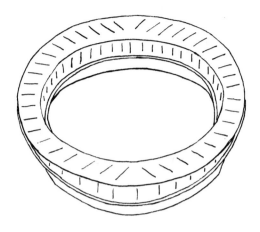

Fig 27

These could be accompanied by verses from St John, Chapter 11, verses 25 and 26.

I am the resurrection and the life,
said the Lord: he that believeth in me,
though he were dead, yet he shall live: and,
whosoever liveth and believeth in me shall
never die.

8
Flowers in Variety

How entrancing it is to wander, unchecked,
through a garden of bright images.

Ernest Bramah

The idea here is to have your church decorated with flowers of
one particular species. Roses or chrysanthemums, dahlias or
sweet peas, carnations or flowering shrubs, or whatever
appeals to you. You may prefer not to be so specific and have
'Annual Flowers' or 'Perennial Flowers'. They are all lovely
titles and the arranging can be free and natural. After all, we
are talking of a festival of flowers and not of floral art.

There is great diversity of colour within the range of a
particular species and equally there is a great diversity in
shape. There are singles, doubles, drawfs, giants, cactus,
spider, ball, pompom, spray and so on. Each flower in Wilda
Woodland's charming cartouche for this chapter heading is a
different variety of rose, and yet they, and many others, are
very different from the 'cabbage' rose for example.

I mentioned in Chapter 1 that visitors are very often
interested in a specific variety of a flower; there is no reason
why known varieties should not be labelled. The labelling can
be reasonably unobtrusive; gardeners are well used to
burrowing in the undergrowth to find name-plates! Together
with the message of your theme and the beauty of the flowers,
labelling the varieties would give a third dimension to your
festival.

For the theme, were you to choose a title like 'Thoughts and Roses', for example, then you are not committed to any particular approach. You can have a poem here, a saying there, a prayer somewhere else, and perhaps as you enter the church and as you leave, a verse from A. G. W. Blunt's hymn, 'Here, Lord, we offer Thee all that is fairest' (see page 47). I use roses in examples in this chapter because they are happy in my garden and do well, so I grow them in profusion and as a result read about them and look at new varieties. The whole 'system' can obviously be applied to any flower you choose to use.

We had a very successful 'Festival of Roses' some years ago. It was a lovely one to plan because of the beautiful colours and being able to choose the most advantageous places to show them was fascinating. An added bonus is the delicious smell in

Fig 28 A little niche, surmounted by a Gothic arch, frames these roses arranged in a wine glass

the church. Why not let the names of the varieties of a particular species of flower, should they be suitable, play a part? With roses, for example, 'Jenny Wren' ('each little flower that opens, each little bird that sings', etc), 'Peace', 'Golden Melody', 'Daybreak', 'Home Sweet Home', 'Celestial', 'Moonlight', 'Rosa Sancta' (St John's Rose), 'Wedding Day' and 'Yesterday' might all help to endorse a meaning.

Yet another angle is the history of the flower and any story, association or symbolism connected with it. It is fabled that Joseph of Arimathea brought the Christian faith to Britain in the year 63, and at Glastonbury he put his staff in the ground and it rooted and became the famous Glastonbury thorn which flowers every Christmas in honour of Christ's birth.

The climbing shrub *passiflora*, the 'Passion Flower', seems to have been given its name by sixteenth-century Spanish missionaries to South Africa. Because of its resemblance to the instruments of the Passion it was obviously a marvellous 'teaching aid'. There are, as with so many of these things, various interpretations of the various meanings. Brewer gives the following:

> The leaf symbolises the spear
> The five petals and five sepals – the ten apostles (Peter who denied and Judas who betrayed being omitted)
> The five anthers – the five wounds
> The tendrils – the scourges
> The column of the ovary – the pillar of the cross
> The stamens – the hammers
> The three stigmas – the three nails
> The filaments within the flower – the crown of thorns
> The calyx – the glory or nimbus
> The white tint – purity
> The blue tint – heaven
> The flower keeps open three days symbolising the three years' ministry.

The rose too is an interesting flower in this respect. In Christian symbolism the rose, as being emblematic of one without peer, is peculiarly appropriated to the Virgin Mary, one of whose titles is 'The Mystical Rose'.

The word 'rosary' used in the sense of a prayer form, is probably derived from the rose and the inward meaning of the word is lucidly explained in the following extract from *Societie of the Rosary*, 1580:

> The name of the Rosary is a most sweet name, for as much as it signifieth no other thing than a spiritual garland made of certain mystical words, as it were roses, taken out of the gospel, offered unto the Virgin of all virgins, the Mother of God. For garlands are ordinarily used to adorn the heads of virgins.

An oasis sausage garland of roses with a prayer within it would be a lovely idea.

Then there are 'Golden Roses', ornaments made of gold in imitation of a spray of roses, one of which contains a receptacle into which is poured balsam and musk. The 'rose' is blessed by the Pope on Laetare Sunday (see page 130) and conferred from time to time on sovereigns and others, churches and cities distinguished for their service.

There are many facets that can be explored using a title in this category. The actual exploring is fascinating and as I said in the first chapter there may well be those in your community who would be delighted to help in this field, even if they do not want to help with the flower arranging. For those, perhaps on their own with time on their hands, exploration in a small way may well lead to an interesting and rewarding pastime. Whatever event we are organising, there is always an opportunity to help someone. Their findings could be included in a hand-out given to the visitors at your festival.

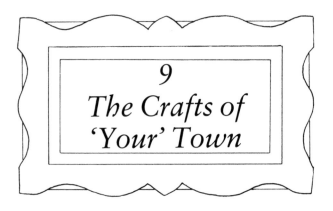

9
The Crafts of 'Your' Town

each for the joy of the working, and
each in his separate star,
shall draw the thing as he sees it for
the God of things as they are

Rudyard Kipling

This is rather an interesting theme to use and, of course, is one that can involve many people either directly, or indirectly, and that is no bad thing. It may also involve people who have previously not shown any interest in church activities, or possibly people of other denominations who will be happy to help.

It is, of course, not essential to call the festival 'The Crafts of "Your" Town'. It may be that you are not a very talented lot! or more likely that your talents lie elsewhere. You can always simply call it a 'Festival of Crafts'.

The idea would be that each craft would show an example of a product of its skill, together with a complementary floral arrangement. I will attempt to suggest ways as how best to incorporate these flowers without always literally doing an arrangement within a container made by a particular craftsman. It would seem appropriate that each craft select their own written accompaniment; again I will give a few suggestions and also how these might be presented. It is not possible to help with the placing of each craft, but I think that the most suitable places will present themselves as you go along.

To begin with, something fairly straightforward . . .

LACE MAKING

As well as showing a pretty piece of lace, I think it would be interesting to show, if possible, some of the tools of the trade; even, perhaps, a cushion upon which some lace was in the process of being made. Imagine, for example, that the cushion was blue and the lace white, then this could be complemented by an arrangement possibly with white gypsophila or hedge parsley, sometimes known as 'Queen Anne's Lace', in a blue container, viewed against a blue background. The lace maker might choose a verse from St Matthew, Chapter 6, verse 28:

> Consider the lilies of the field,
> how they grow, they toil not, neither
> do they spin

This would be attractive in an oval shape with an edging of lacy white flowers. You would obviously need a coloured background to show the white flowers; blue would link up well. Either you could use a series of containers poked through the cardboard like those used for a single flower (Figure 23, page 53), or paint the back of the plywood board used for a sausage garland (Figure 25, page 57), having drilled holes around the edge before affixing the oasis sausage. The flowers can then be poked from the front through the holes into an the oasis on the back. The oval cardboard with the writing can then be stuck directly on to the board, as any leakage from the oasis sausage will take place behind rather than onto the writing.

WOODWORK, CARPENTRY, WOOD TURNING, FURNITURE MAKING, etc

These could come under separate headings if space permits, or all together. That is up to you. As well as any objects you may import, inevitably you will have things of beauty in the church for at least one of these headings. We have a fifteenth-century chest and the old wood in its natural state is a marvellous setting for flowers. You may have a carved rood screen, or a chair, or particularly interesting pew ends to which you wish to draw attention. It is no bad thing that we should all appreciate and think about the superb craftsmanship that we have in so many of our churches, and perhaps some details of their history could be incorporated in a leaflet. Flowers used in ways discussed in Chapter 3 could help to enhance their beauty.

A woodworker would perhaps write his 'text' on wood and the lines by A. J. Kilmer might appeal to him:

Poems are made by fools like me
but only God can make a tree.

CHINA OR POTTERY MAKING

Here, of course, one has to interpret according to the type of pottery or porcelain you are showing. Perhaps blue and white, perhaps polychrome, or perhaps floral, in which case you could copy the design with real flowers. Robert Browning's

Time's wheel runs back or stops,
Potter and clay endure

might be chosen here. It would be rather fun if you could find a large oval meat plate with a pretty floral border, and to use it on a plate stand as a vehicle for the writing. This could be done on an oval card cut to fit the base of the plate and fixed onto it by using double-sided sticky tape.

WHEELWRIGHT

I have really included this because I think that a wheel is such a lovely vehicle for displaying flowers. Between each spoke can be arranged all the colours of the rainbow or shades of one colour or what you will. Also, it is a golden opportunity for a break in the shape and manner of the flower arrangement. Were you to choose a suitable writing, then it could be written around the felloe of the wheel. How about

Invention breeds Invention.

Ralph Waldo Emerson

COOKERY

We all have to eat and as we are reminded by endless books and glossy magazines, there is a great skill in cookery. To bring this craft to our floral wavelength, apart from the herbs, which from early days have helped to make the food more edible and digestible, there are some vegetables which are most attractive and could well make an unusual arrangement.

Were you to take a leaf out of the Reverend Kilvert's diary, you could write your words in wheat ears, perhaps not on red flannel but instead in a bed of emerald green parsley. 'Give us this day our daily bread' would be very eye-catching written across a sloping windowsill.

SILVERSMITH AND GOLDSMITH

A dark background, or better still, a red or blue curtain, would show your silver and gold off best. There are obviously many items you could use including, if you have one, a highly polished silver tray propped up on its edge. In front of it you could have a suitably sized arrangement reflected in the tray behind. Other interesting pieces could also be shown. Alternatively, you may have some beautiful birds cast in silver or some object which portrays the silversmith's skill; alongside could be an all silver arrangement in a silver container, perhaps a candlestick.

With gold, I doubt that one could produce a tray or even a candlestick! More likely a gold filigree bracelet or necklace which would have to be looked down upon as would a circlet of golden flowers alongside.

An apt quotation would be Proverbs, Chapter 25, verse 11:

A word fitly spoken is like apples of
gold in pictures of silver.

On the same principle as the meat plate, this could be shown on a silver tray with the embossed edge acting as a frame. A tray with two carrying handles could have a posy in each handle. If the tray has no handles, then one rose affixed (Figure 23, page 53) would alleviate the starkness.

WROUGHT IRON

It may well be that your church already contains some work of this type in the form of altar rails, or a door, or candlesticks, or even a flowerstand. If there is a wrought-iron fixture or fitting, then obviously this must a focus of attention and complemented by any other work you may import. An arrangement either on a wrought-iron pedestal or in a wrought-iron candle holder would look equally well. I think for this craft I would choose the quotation by Kipling used at the beginning of this chapter. Were you to use a wrought-iron fireguard to fix it to you would have a ready-built stand, which, depending upon its design, could be decorated by various means. See pages 32–3.

PICTURE FRAMING

This craft rather speaks for itself. An old gold frame and a suitably proportioned natural arrangement within and you have recreated a Dutch masterpiece. The writing again could be framed. How about Thomas Dekker,

Honest labour bears a lovely face.

THATCHING

It might be difficult not only to persuade a thatcher to come and thatch something in the church, but also to persuade the incumbent and churchwardens to allow him to do so! Perhaps you could resort to bringing into the church some object already thatched, such as a bird-feeding table. If, however, you could arrange for some proper thatching, you could always thatch the entrance to the churchyard and create a sort of lychgate (if you haven't one already) which would act as a wonderful advertisement, particularly if you filled it with bright red geraniums. Alternatively, if you were able to do something within the church, how about thatching a roof to the pulpit? You could probably contrive a window box and have flowers up the pulpit steps to complete your summerhouse.

The card for your written word could be shaped like the gable end of a house and have a little thatch over it. A prayer might be suitable here:

O Lord! thou knowest how busy
I must be this day; if I forget
thee, do not thou forget me.

Sir Jacob Astley

BASKET AND TRUG MAKING

A picnic-type basket with the lid raised, or a cherry basket, or many other sorts of baskets look lovely with flowers in them. Obviously, one has to be careful not to obscure the art of the basket maker.

Trug making is a separate skill but, like the basket, can be used as a container. In the case of the trug, however, the flowers would be best arranged to appear to be almost lying in it as if they had just been picked. Again, something like a flower basket, laid on its side, could act as a frame for the words from Exodus, Chapter 20, verses 9 and 10,

Six days shalt thou labour, and do
all thy work:
But the seventh day *is* the sabbath
of the Lord thy God.

GLASS MAKING

All churches have windows and whether clear or stained glass, they are all part of the glass maker's skill and their sills pose a good site for the trade of glass making. If you have details as to the age or any other feature of the window, do draw attention to them; people are interested.

You may have some engraved glass or cut glass or very special blown glass to exhibit. The flower side of this exhibit would be well shown within glass, with perhaps just one lovely flower floating in a glass container that shows the transparency of the glass itself. You could perhaps contrive to have the wording read through glass or reflected by it.

For now we see through a glass,
darkly; but then face to face: now I
know in part; but then shall I know
even as also I am known.

1st Corinthians, Chapter 13, verse 12

I am sure that you will have thought of many suitable crafts in keeping with your locality. Should you still not have found as many as you would like, how about weaving, sculpture, spinning, boat-building, needlework, printing, leatherwork, bonsai, or just plain horticulture. To recap, where there are interesting tools of the trade that can be shown, do show them whenever possible.

It is good to have several dimensions to any exhibition. You have the tools, the finished product, the complementary flowers and the written word.

10
The Language of Flowers

Its symbols smile upon the land
Wrought by nature's wonderous hand
And in their silent beauty speak
Of Life and Joy to those who seek
For Love Divine and sunny hours
In the language of the flowers.

Anon

It is perhaps helpful to consider briefly the history of the meanings and associations given to flowers. Man has always been aware of the wonders of nature and of its changing seasons; it was only natural, therefore, that pagan man should be in awe of the unknown powers responsible for the natural world. Some flowers were seen as omens of good or evil, others were recognised for their medicinal powers, and many others were associated with the gods and goddesses of mythology.

When Augustine and his monks came to Britain as missionaries, the Pope wisely instructed them that for the converts there should be no sudden break with the past; but rather that pagan rites were to be merged with Christian rites, thus grafting new ideas on to the old practices and gradually weaning the people from their pagan thinking. So it was with flowers, and those 'belonging' to mythological figures were gradually transferred, many to the Virgin Mary and many others to the saints. This allotment of flowers to the saints was, by and large, a practical one, namely, whichever flower was flowering nearest to the date of a particular saint's day was sensibly appropriated to that saint. For example, the Christmas rose was allotted to St Agnes (21 January), and also doubled for the feast of St Paul's conversion (25 January). A list of the saints and their flowers is at the end of this book.

As time passed and the Christian message was received, so the need for this association diminished. So too did the list of saints, and possibly it is their virtues that remain in connection with the meanings of flowers, together with the medicinal and other associations that have come down through the ages. For whatever reason a particular flower has acquired a particular meaning, it is easy to see how many variations on these meanings have come about. Your source of information may give a different interpretation of a flower from that given by my source. It doesn't really matter; they are all interesting, and although, surely, they must not be taken too seriously, would nevertheless make an attractive idea for a flower festival. I would recommend that you avoid flowers with trivial meanings, otherwise it could be difficult to give much depth to the message of the festival. What we are actually doing is employing a gimmick, if you like, to give a message through our flowers by using an ancient 'language' of their own. To give the names of the flowers, and their meanings, would therefore be necessary.

Many of these flowers are not easy to display on their own. Thoughts and flowers could be grouped and then their placing would add a third dimension. For example:

Rosemary	Remembrance
Achillea	War
White Bellflower	Gratitude
Nasturtium	Patriotism

and all thoughts connected with war memorials.

| Reeds | Music |
| White Pinks | Talent |

would be well placed by the organ.

Moss	Maternal love
White Scilla	Sweet innocence
Wood Sorrel	Joy, natural tenderness
White Daisy	Innocence

are certainly thoughts that could centre around the font where their children are baptised.

There are endless combinations of ideas that will come to you. Alternatively, you may prefer to take one thought and develop that for instance,

| Ivy | Everlasting life |

together with the passage from St John, Chapter 3, verse 16,

> God so loved the world that he gave his
> only begotten son, to the end that all
> that believe in him should not perish but
> have everlasting life.

There are many beautiful ivies, some variegated, some not, which would make an attractive decoration spiralled around a pillar or post or would certainly be very meaningful above the altar.

The white daisy, innocence, and the passage from St Mark, Chapter 10, verse 14,

> Suffer the little children to come unto me and
> forbid them not: for of such is the kingdom of God.

Large white daisies in the font (if your vicar allows you to do so) with daisy chains round its base and festooned around it, with garlands of bigger daisies and so on (Figure 29).

The lilac or the lily of the valley, humility, and the collect from the first Sunday in advent:

Fig 29 Ivy (depicting everlasting life) and white daisies (depicting innocence) make an attractive decoration on this unusual font

Almighty God, give us grace that we may cast
away the works of darkness and put upon us
the armour of light, now in the time of
this mortal life, in which thy Son Jesus
Christ came to visit us in great humility.

The rose, associated with Christ and with the Virgin Mary, is given the meaning of love. From St John, Chapter 15, verse 12,

Love one another as I have loved you.

Together with such a 'text' it would be necessary to show not only the flower, or flowers, involved, but their meaning. Were you using a group of four, as in the first example given, rosemary, achillea, white bellflower, nasturtium, one must not assume that the visitor knows which is which. It would seem sense to have a specimen of each, and its meaning, to act as a sort of decoration or 'border' to a text. It would certainly add to the attraction of the whole presentation.

You will think of a variety of ideas, whether taking thoughts singly or grouping them or both. Here is a list of flowers and their meanings which may be of help:

Flowering Almond	Hope
Amaryllis	Pride
Azalea	Temperance
Bluebell	Constancy
Chrystanthemum	Truth
Columbine	Resolution
Cowslip	Pensiveness
Crocus	Mirth
Daffodil	Chivalry (the Lent Lily)
White Daisy	Innocence
Dock	Patience
Fern	Sincerity
Geranium (oak leaved)	True friendship
Geranium (scarlet)	Comforting
Heliotrope	Devotion
Hibiscus	Delicate beauty
Holly	Foresight
Ivy	Everlasting life
Lilac	Humility
Lily of the Valley	Purity, humility
Magnolia	Dignity
Pansy	Thoughts
White Pink	Talent
Reeds	Music
Rose	Love
Rosemary	Remembrance

11
Famous Sayings

Never, no never, did nature say one thing
and wisdom another

Edmund Burke

To me there is little point using this theme unless one is prepared to use sayings of some substance. To use adages such as 'a stitch in time saves nine' doesn't really give a very profound message! The sayings of the philosophers are perhaps the most thought provoking; on the other hand, one does not want to make it too intense. Indeed, there is absolutely no reason why a touch of humour should not be added. A variety, therefore, would strike a good balance.

It may not, in every case, be easy to have an obvious connection between the saying and the flowers. This isn't of great moment because the flowers will be lovely and if the saying has a message and prompts thought, then the lack of apparent connection is not of prime importance.

The choice of sayings needs to be given considerable thought. To illustrate to those helping you the concept that you have in mind, and to assist them in choosing their own sayings, you will need to give a few examples. Begin with better known ones whose interpretation is straightforward and lead up to what one might describe as the 'deeper' ones. If you like, to start with, you could use examples from the two themes already discussed, 'Hymns' and 'Poetry with Flowers'. Here are a few further examples to illustrate these ideas.

A thing of beauty is a joy for ever:
Its loveliness increases: it will never
Pass into nothingness.

John Keats, 1795–1821

You could use this with a dried arrangement which included dried seed heads: these would illustrate the 'never pass into nothingness'.

Never in the field of human conflict was
so much owed by so many to so few.

Sir Winston Churchill, 1874–1965

There are obviously many ways in which this could be done. I would use annuals; perhaps sweet peas as an example, a huge number of them, with a very few seed pods scattered alongside.

A good book is the best of friends, the same
to-day and forever.

Martin Tupper, 1810–89

I don't think the flowers you use matter. It is the placing in this case that is more meaningful, either upon or under the lectern.

When you have nothing to say – say nothing.

Charles Caleb Colton, 1780?–1832

How about an arrangement of antirrhinums (snapdragons).

Never take anything for granted.

Benjamin Disraeli, 1804–81

A lovely collection of flowers is all that is needed to make that point.

Nothing costs us so dear as a waste of time.

> Diogenes, born *c* 412BC

One is tempted to do any arrangement connected with Diogenes in a large earthenware jar. He is purported to have taken up residence in such a jar. The original 'think tank' I presume!

> There must be a beginning of any great matter,
> but the continuing unto the end, until it be
> thoroughly finished yields the true glory.
>
> Sir Francis Drake, 1540?–96

This one I should place at the beginning.

> There is an art of reading as well as an art
> of thinking and an art of writing.
>
> Isaac D'Israeli, 1776–1848

This, I think, should be fairly early on as a sort of hint as to what to look for.

> The salvation of mankind lies only in making
> everything the concern of all.
>
> Alexander Solzhenitsyn, 1918– (Nobel lecture, 1970)

I would do an arrangement with as many different flowers and foliages as I could muster – probably on a pedestal.

> The child can see further on the shoulders
> of the man.
>
> Aristotle, *c* 444–*c* 380BC

This refers to the increase of man's knowledge as each

generation learns from the previous one. I would feel inclined to use modern, really beautiful roses, giving the name and the parentage of each rose to show how it has been bred and improved.

Here is another one to think about –

Sow an act and you reap a habit. Sow a habit
and you reap a character. Sow a character and
you reap a destiny.

Charles Reade 1814–84

One could go on and on citing sayings from the Bible. You would probably want to choose ones making points that seem to be lacking in your other sayings, so as to strike a balance.

Unto the pure all things *are* pure.

Titus, Chapter 1, verse 15

perhaps with an all white arrangement.

A merry heart maketh a cheerful countenance.

Proverbs, Chapter 15, verse 13

placed beside a colourful sunny arrangement.

He that hath ears to hear, let him hear.

St Mark, Chapter 4, verse 9

trumpet-shaped flowers perhaps?

Man shall not live by bread alone
but by every word that proceedeth
out of the mouth of God.

St Matthew, Chapter 4, verse 4

A combination of an arrangement incorporating corn and

done on the lectern is an idea for this one; and lastly a saying attributed to St Francis of Assisi –

It is in giving that we receive.

Fig 30 A saying attributed to Saint Francis is ringed with flowers using the method illustrated in Figure 25

12
God's
Garden

God Almightie first planted a garden.
And, indeed, it is the purest of all humane pleasures.

Francis Bacon

Planning this is a veritable field day for all your budding
Gertrude Jekylls and Capability Browns! You are literally
planning a garden or many gardens and, like any landscape
gardener, must make use of and incorporate the features on
your site: the steps for your rock garden, pillars and posts for
shrubs and standard roses, wide aisles for herbaceous borders.
You have the making of pergolas, windows for window boxes,
side chapels for rose gardens and so on. You will need lots of
willing helpers, but the joy of this title is the amount that can
be done by people who are unused to flower arranging and,
therefore, shy of helping.

There are several ways of depicting this theme. I would
choose to have a plurality of gardens selected with a historical
bias. You would need for visitors a brief explanatory leaflet as
people tend to get bored if given too much to read.

THE GARDEN OF GETHSEMANE

No pageant of gardens in a church would be complete without
the Garden of Gethsemane and within the garden the

reconstruction of a stone tomb with the stone closing the tomb 'rolled away'. Moss could conceal containers of small flowers around and between the stones while the rest of the garden could contain taller flowers and shrubs. A suitable 'text' on the resurrection and its significance for us would complete this garden sited in the sanctuary.

GARDEN OF EDEN

Were your festival in the apple season, then you might choose to include the Garden of Eden. The branch of a crab apple tree, fully laden with deep red apples, could be the focal point and would be a good accompaniment to a thought on temptation! Clumps of wild flowers in a mossy bed would complete your wild garden.

HERB GARDEN

In the early Christian church herbs were used in rites and ceremonies and every English cathedral and monastery had its herb garden. They were used medicinally too and there are many legends associated with herbs, the basis of these doubtless going back to Hippocrates (*c* 460BC), 'The Father of Medicine', and many of these early herbal remedies have come down to us and are often referred to as 'old wives' tales'. The first really great English *Herbal* was produced in 1597 by John Gerrard, a surgeon, and with whom we associate the physic garden. Herbal remedies were much used by physicians until the eighteenth century and of course today certain drugs are still obtained from these natural sources.

The culinary use of herbs reached its climax during the sixteenth century, the age of the Elizabethan herb garden. A well stocked garden might include as many as sixty different herbs for use medicinally, for cooking and for scents. The layout of such a garden would have been in an often intricate pattern of borders possibly edged with lavender, rosemary or box.

A potted history of herbs would need to be included in your

visitors' hand-out and their various usages could also be included or briefly indicated beside the relevant herb in your garden.

Reference as to how such a garden should be laid out is not difficult to find and there is no doubt that the brick or stone floors of so many of our churches would provide the ready-made paths between the formally laid out herb beds.

MARY GARDENS

Idealistic gardens depicted in art during the Middle Ages were known as 'Mary Gardens'. If you have a suitably placed statue of the Virgin Mary, then this would be an attractive idea to emulate. Examples of these gardens can be seen in medieval tapestries, paintings and manuscripts. Mary is usually shown seated in a walled garden; in the garden a rose or perhaps a tree in blossom; raised beds behind her might contain iris, daisies and, of course, Madonna lilies, with, in the foreground, perhaps lily of the valley or cowslips.

SACRISTAN'S GARDEN

Very real and equally practical gardens were the gardens kept by the sacristans, certainly up until the time of the Reformation. From these the sacristan provided flowers and foliage for use in the church at the various festivals. In such a garden you would have a wealth of interest for the visitor in the various uses of the trees and flowers that would have been grown in it. Many of these have already been mentioned in Chapter 1 and elsewhere in this book. Obviously, when we are talking of the festivals of the church's year, we are covering a whole season in the garden and there would, therefore, be practical difficulties to produce everything at any one time; however, by dint of a bit of cheating, you could probably manage! Holly, ivy, cedar and yew are always available. You can buy extremely realistic holly berries to attach to your sprigs of holly. It is often possible to buy imported daffodils (Lent lilies). The willow (which in this country we substitute for the palm), is still a willow whatever time of the year it may be; probably the summer, so roses and Madonna lilies would also be available, as would rosemary which had a variety of uses, not least for weddings when the bride's attendants had rosemary 'tied about their sleeves' and a 'goodly branch' of rosemary was carried before the bride in the 'bride-cup'. Possibly too the sacristan had some vines (a little cheating here too might help). Any of the saints' flowers that were out at the time of your festival could also be included, together with a card giving the name of the flower and the saint associated with it.

An explanation of the usage of the various trees and flowers would be needed, either alongside or under the heading of 'Sacristan's Garden' in your leaflet for visitors. Such a garden could well have included herbs or even a herb garden. It would link up well to have these two gardens adjacent or, if space were limited, combined.

GARDEN OF REMEMBRANCE

Most churches would probably have somewhere suitable for a 'Garden of Remembrance'. For this a bed, or beds, of red roses enclosed by a low evergreen 'hedge' would be an idea.

GARDEN FOR THE DISABLED

We are all familiar with gardens for the disabled with raised beds easily accessible to someone in a wheelchair. The front pews in some cases might lend themselves to this purpose; if not I am sure that you could find a suitable place. Happily you may not have any disabled in your community, in which case there would be little point in including this garden as there would be no one to make it.

There are numerous other ideas for gardens that you could think of and the bigger your church, and the more side chapels and so on you have, the more gardens you could include. There are scented gardens or 'bee gardens', white gardens, silver gardens, rose gardens, terrace gardens, cottage gardens, knot gardens, sunken gardens, rock gardens, Italian gardens, children's gardens and, if you are sufficiently enterprising, why not a water garden.

In a church within which you can have small gardens of this nature, because you are able to ring the changes by their different sizes, colourings and contents, you create a change of mood and the opportunity to convey a different message in each. At the same time you are stimulating thought and making the visitor eager to see more.

Each garden would have its own written thought. Rather than having cards, upon which these thoughts are written, decorated in the manner suggested in previous chapters, it might seem in keeping to have them stuck into the 'earth' or 'grass' as it were, like the notices one sees in parks asking you to keep off the grass or not to pick the flowers.

With this theme the organisation has to be very good, otherwise on the decorating day everyone will be getting in everyone else's way. There is little doubt, however, that given a suitable church, this is one of the loveliest of all themes, both in its idea and by the effect it creates.

13
The
Seasons

In seed time learn, in harvest teach,
in winter enjoy

William Blake

Like so many maxims applied to plant life, the above
quotation from Blake's *The Marriage of Heaven and Hell*
could equally apply to human life. Using flowers not only to
give pleasure, but to say something and to give a message, is
certainly not difficult therefore when thinking of the seasons.

Whether you choose to depict all four seasons at the same
festival, or to have one (perhaps in conjunction with other
churches), in each of the four seasons in the year, or simply to
have one only of the four is obviously up to you. Should you
elect to depict all four seasons at the same time, then you
would probably have to buy flowers for at least one of them,
depending of course on the time of year you choose for your
festival. It would probably help to use dried flowers for winter.

SPRING

A. C. Swinburne wrote 'Blossom by blossom the spring begins'

and any arrangement depicting the spring must surely be light
and delicate and full of the gaiety of youth. Use as many spring
flowers and blossoms as you can, separately and together, to
create an overall effect that will be beautiful and full of hope.
Thoughts on spring are usually those of sowing seeds and of
learning.

> Be not deceived; God is not mocked:
> for whatsoever a man soweth, that
> shall he also reap.

Galtaians, Chapter 6, verse 7

Also of renewed faith and hope –

> Now faith is the substance of things hoped for,
> the evidence of things not seen.

Hebrews, Chapter 11, verse 1

You will find your own quotations to use, to say what you
want to say. In order to illustrate the idea, however, I shall give
two examples for each season.

SUMMER

Take advantage of the many hues of summer and the
abundance of flowers of every variety that summer brings:
sweet-scented lilies, sweet peas, carnations, roses. Fill the
church with perfume and flowers in profusion. Blake leaves
summer out of his quotation, but you might fill the gap in one
way. I would insert 'In summer think and experience' and have
thoughts at a summer festival in that vein.

> Experience is the child of thought,
> and thought is the child of action . . .

Benjamin Disraeli

Again, that marvellous quotation from Tennyson's *Ulysses*,
this time including two more lines:

Yet all experience is an arch wherethro'
Gleams that untravelled world, whose margin fades
For ever and for ever when I move.
How dull it is to pause, to make an end,
To rust unburnished, not to shine in use.

A lovely bright arrangement around an archway and seen as
the visitor leaves the church would seem appropriate here.

AUTUMN

All the serene shades of autumn, the bronzes, the golds, the
fruits, the berries, the ripened corn, can all harmoniously
blend together, like a harvest festival.

Blake suggests 'in harvest teach'. This might be the most
suitable festival of the four for the verse from Genesis, Chapter
8, verse 22:

> While the earth remaineth, seed time and harvest, and cold
> and heat, and summer and winter, and day and night shall
> not cease.

Lines from Bishop Thomas Ken's hymn would seem well
placed in the autumn of man's life,

> Teach me to live, that I may dread
> The grave as little as my bed.

WINTER

Is it not wonderful that some of the most delicate looking of
our shrubs and flowers are those that bloom in winter? The
lovely fragrant viburnums, yellow jasmine, *Helleborus niger*,
Iris stylosa, snowdrops, cyclamen, aconites, some varieties of
rhododendron, and dainty blossom of *Prunus subhirtella
autumnalis*. Besides these, we must not forget the berries, the
evergreens, the coloured bark of the dogwoods, and the dainty
winter clematis. How we delight in them in the cold winter
months and how right Blake was when he said 'in winter enjoy'.

Verses from F. S. Pierpoint's hymn 'For the beauty of the
Earth' placed around the church would be one idea here;
another perhaps from the Book of Revelation, Chapter 4,
verse 11:

> Thou art worthy, O Lord, to receive glory and honour and
> power; for thou hast created all things, and for thy pleasure
> they are and were created.

Portraying all the seasons at the same festival will call for a
decision as to which season is placed where in your church. On
the basis of the Blake quotation at the beginning of this
chapter, I would start with youth, the first of the four seasons,
and the first to be seen: spring, therefore, at the back of the
church and around the area of the font; summer would then
occupy the nave, the centre of the church; autumn, the
chancel, the area of the pulpit and the lectern, the places of
teaching; leaving winter to enjoy the peace and serenity of the
sanctuary.

At such a festival, somewhere in the church the verses from
Ecclesiastes, Chapter 3, beginning at verse 1, would seem at
home:

> To everything there is a season, and a time to every purpose
> under the heaven.

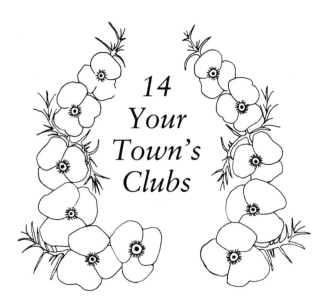

14
Your
Town's
Clubs

Our lives, like bells, while changing,
An ordered course pursue;
Through joys and sorrows ranging,
May all those lives ring true

H. C. Wilder

More than any other theme, this one, I believe, probably involves the greatest cross-section of your community. Many of these people are possibly not members of your church or indeed churchgoers at all. Undoubtedly, the more people you involve, the more people they, in turn, will attract to come to your festival.

Not all parishes, even big ones, necessarily have many clubs and societies, but they may have large churches. Why not extend your area to the whole town, or district or benefice? People would probably be very happy to join in. When you think about it, there is a great deal that can be done under this heading.

The general idea is that every club, society or group would each portray themselves using flowers, and at the same time select a helpful thought that would tie in with their particular purpose. It could even be that the club had a motto that would be appropriate to use. Each activity would, therefore, have a suitable place allocated to them. How this is done is your individual problem! It should not prove too great a worry: perhaps you have a Mothers' Union banner permanently displayed in the church and that area could be theirs. The over sixties club might choose to have gold flowers or evergreens, so an area that asks for this colouring (and doesn't involve climbing about) would be theirs; the History Society might be placed near a brass or an effigy of someone famous; the British Legion, wherever your memorial is; the bell-ringers under the tower, and so on.

One cannot simply designate an area for use by a particular society and hope for the best. There are always a few overriding factors (Chapter 2), for instance, some liaison of colour if 'A' is to complement 'B' and so on. This may well help to solve some of the placing. Again, I think that there should be some overall pattern, to the extent that all the headings, assuming you have them, telling the visitor that it is the WI or the Boys' Brigade or whatever, are uniform. If each exhibit were to design their own label, denoting which club they were, in a different way, it could spoil the continuity and oneness of the theme.

In order to help people formulate their own ideas, it is always a good practice to have a few examples of what can be done. This is undoubtedly the best way of getting people on your wavelength and to stimulate thought.

Here are a few examples that may help.

THE BELL-RINGERS

The flowers used for this would be bell-like flowers and the arrangement could perhaps be tiered, using the largest bells at the foot of the arrangement, working up to the smallest at the top. Under the bell tower would seem the obvious place for this to be. The quotation at the beginning of this chapter would be a good one to choose and around it a painted cartouche of different sized bells and their ropes, ringing this way and that.

THE BRITISH LEGION

Red poppies, red roses and rosemary would be suitable flowers to use in an arrangement, perhaps in the form of a wreath. The memorial window, or by the roll of honour would be the natural place for the British Legion. For a quotation I would think the best choice would be the words of Lawrence Binyon:

> They shall not grow old, as we that are left grow old:
> Age shall not weary them or the years condemn.
> At the going down of the sun and in the morning
> We will remember them.

The words could be framed with a cartouche of poppies saved from 'Poppy Day'.

THE FLOWER CLUB

There would be no significance, in this case, attached to the choice of flowers; the placing too would probably not matter, affording the opportunity to use one of the 'in-between' areas, provided it allowed sufficient space possibly to show two or three stages of an arrangement 'under construction', together with the finished product. The first verse of C. A. Alington's hymn

> Lord of beauty, thine the splendour
> Shewn in earth and sky and sea,
> Burning sun and moonlight tender,
> Hill and river, flower and tree:
> Lest we fail our praise to render
> Touch our eyes that they may see.

would look well encircled by a circlet of wired flowers, made with the florist's skill, and stapled on to the cardboard.

THE FOOTBALL SUPPORTERS' CLUB

The flowers or foliage here would be chosen in the club colours. An arrangement done in the shape of a football would be appropriate. This would look best suspended in a doorway or archway using oasis in a hanging basket.

Lines from Grantland Rice's 'Alumnus Football' would be a good choice:

For when the One Great Scorer comes
To write against your name,
He marks – not that you won or lost –
But how you played the game.

written in white lettering upon a black card, the whole designed to look like a scoreboard.

THE OVER SIXTIES CLUB

The natural choice of flowers and foliage here would seem to be golden flowers and evergreens. The placing is immaterial, provided the members are not required to climb about to reach inaccessible places. The sanctuary might prove a good place.

A verse by Christina Rossetti would seem apt:

And dreaming through the twilight
That does not rise nor set,
Haply I may remember,
And haply may forget.

MOTHERS' UNION

Madonna lilies, were they in season, would be a good choice of flower, placed to complement the Mothers' Union banner if you have one. If you have no lilies and no banner, then pink, blue and white flowers around the font would be another idea. An excerpt from the Mothers' Union Prayer would make a fitting quotation:

Grant that by prayer and worship we may lead our families in holiness and purity of life, and help others to do the same;

the floral decoration could be in keeping with the flowers in your arrangement.

THE DISABLED PERSONS' CLUB

The choice of flowers in this case would not be significant but the position all important. You would need to select a place, or places, easily accessible to people in wheelchairs. Small baskets, made by the blind, and attached to pew ends might be the answer. It would obviously be important that each person selected their own flowers independently in order that each basket of flowers differed from the others and was totally individual. It is difficult to guess what this club might choose for a quotation but were I to select for them, I think that the whole of Milton's sonnet 'Upon His Blindness' would be very meaningful, set out on two cards, one to be written in braille and the other decorated, possibly with pressed flowers, by those members unable to get to the church.

Fig 31 This winter arrangement of white *Viburnam fragrans* and *V. tinus*, *Daphne retusa*, *Helleborus niger* and *Prunus subhurtilla autumnalis* together with yellow jasmine and gold eleagnus, complements the gold embroidery on the kneelers while at the same time detracting from the plain pew ends

THE NEEDLEWORK GUILD

The choice of flowers would very largely depend upon the placing of this guild in the church. Possibly near an embroidered hanging, or flowers embroidered on kneelers, in which case you might wish to emulate colours and flowers. If you are not tied in this way, then a patchwork of colour would be lovely. Rather than write the chosen quotation, this guild could work it in cross stitch and embroider decorations around it in the manner of a sampler. The needlewoman would probably appreciate a short text: for example, 'God is Love'.

HISTORY SOCIETY

History is not of course confined to endless lists of dates of kings, battles and prime ministers, such as some of us were led to believe at school! It is broadly 'the methodical record of a country, person, or thing'. The 'thing' in our case being flowers, your history society might choose to pursue this line, unless of course there is some very outstanding feature in your church which would be of more interest.

Were they to elect to take the history of flowers, this could be presented in a variety of ways. Firstly, there is the origin of an individual flower and the history of its development. The dahlia would be a good example of this. Alternatively, one could trace the history of the use of a particular flower, or flowers, and whether they were used in folk lore, in rites and ceremonies, in medicine, symbolically, and so on. The flowers of the saints might be incorporated here (see the list at the end of the book), together with the history of the transference of these flowers to them (Chapter 10). A good example to use would be St John the Baptist to whom flowers of light and sunshine were dedicated. The sun depressing darkness symbolised the Baptist who proclaimed light. Flowers with large sun-shaped heads such as the moon daisy and various members of the chrysanthemum family, as well as other yellow flowers, in particular St John's Wort (*hypericum*), were associated with him. Gladys Taylor in her fascinating book *The Saints and their Flowers* writes,

> In the days when witches and sorcery held sway over men's minds St John's Wort was regarded as a magical herb. On the eve of his feast [St John the Baptist] it was picked with great ceremony and hung up in windows as a protection against evil spirits, spectres, phantoms, storms and thunder. It was burnt in the midsummer fires for the same preventative purpose and worn or carried by people as a guard against witchcraft. In addition, the healing virtues of one kind of the plant were so great that it was called Tutsan – from the French toute saine, all heal.

Perhaps a quote from Friedrich von Schiller's first lecture on becoming a professor of history would fit here:

> The world's history is the world's judgement.

It could be decorated with a border of as many saints' flowers as were available, together with the name of the flower and the saint to whom it was appropriated.

There are clubs and societies whose subjects are described elsewhere in this book: Poetry Society – see Chapter 5; Rose, Dahlia, Chrysanthemum Societies – see Chapter 8; Painting Group – see page 122; Music/Choral Societies – see Chapter 4 and page 117; Nature Conservation Society – see Chapter 15. Don't forget the Women's Institute, the Girl Guides, the Boys' Brigade, the Youth Club, the Horticultural and Agricultural Societies, and finally miniature flowers for the Model Makers.

There are, of course, many more clubs, groups and societies than I have mentioned here and the more you can incorporate, the merrier. With a festival of this nature those helping with a particular club's decorating take pleasure in seeing all the other clubs' contributions and reading their messages. Everyone, therefore, gives to everyone else.

15
Wild
Flowers

When daisies pied and violets blue
And lady-smocks all silver white
and cuckoo-buds of yellow hue
Do paint the meadows with delight

William Shakespeare

This theme has become an increasingly difficult one to do thanks to the combined efforts of the councils' cutting the roadside verges and sprays drifting onto verges from neighbouring fields. However, with the council spending cuts in our part of the world, we have again been able to enjoy the flowers, as the first cut of the season has been withdrawn. (It is, of course, possible, if you have a particularly lovely stretch of verge, not on a dangerous corner, to apply through the proper channels and postpone the cutting, council spending cuts or not.) Tremendous work is being done by many conservation groups, and given the support they deserve, the survival of our wild flowers could be insured.

Obviously, there are still places where wild flowers can be found in profusion, not least amongst them country churchyards. It is not uncommon for over a hundred species to be recorded on one acre of ground, particularly where they have escaped modern 'weed' killers and been kept cut by traditional methods, thus allowing the semi-natural vegetation to remain comparatively unchanged since the graveyard was enclosed. Interestingly enough it appears that the graveyards, enclosed say in Victorian times, where there are still areas as yet undisturbed by burials, are possibly the richest in wild flowers. The soil in medieval graveyards has been turned over many times, and whereas it has been enriched in the process, many gems have been lost if rough turfs have not been replaced but instead the area levelled and reseeded with grass seed.

We have always followed the system of replacing the turfs; however the jolly young man from the Co-op, who digs to the accompaniment of his transistor and has taken over from his traditional, now retired, predecessor, is determined that we should mend our ways and tidy the place up! I don't somehow feel that he will have much success in converting us and the blankets of white violets and cowslips will remain unshaken.

It is in country churches, therefore, that this theme would seem to be at home. June is our best month for wild flowers and, obviously, with this title, the date must be chosen to suit the flowers. The other way about will get you nowhere!

Naming the flowers could prove rather a problem as one tends to use so many different flowers in one arrangement. There are, however, some very splendid illustrated charts available and it might add interest to put these up.

How you use the flowers will vary with each individual. It is occasionally effective to have an arrangement using only one particular flower. An arrangement of cowslips (or a 'cowslip ball') or of marsh marigolds, of foxgloves, poppies or harebells and many, many others can be lovely. Alternatively, it is interesting perhaps to use flowers in families, when of course the family name would be given. Variety is the spice of effect in arrangements with wild flowers. You may be very surprised at the delightful and interesting festival you can create.

You have probably gathered by now that I am a lover of poetry and prose, probably because it says for me what I cannot say for myself. It is a good idea sometimes to have a heading or 'leader' as you enter the church. How about,

The Fairest Flowers o' the Season.

Shakespeare, *The Winter's Tale*

Like 'Flowers in Variety' the title of your festival could be in similar vein. 'Wild Flowers and Wisdom', or again, 'Thoughts and Wild Flowers'. A relevant thought here, a prayer there, a truth somewhere else, and so on. The cards upon which these thoughts are written could be in a variety of shapes, as suited the words. To identify the flowers used in the arrangement, a floral decoration of those flowers, pressed and with their names alongside, could decorate the writing and at the same time would add a third dimension for the visitor.

With every subject there are many facets that can be explored for added interest. The historical approach, perhaps here a matter for the ecologist, would seem particularly relevant with wild flowers. He can tell us, for example, how the white campion arrived with agriculture to join, and in the course of time largely overcome, the native red campion which grew in wooded areas. Again, there is the medicinal use of flowers. The early herbalists advocated the eating of lady's smock (the cuckoo flower) to strengthen the heart; while dried colt's foot leaves were used to make a cough linctus. Today the drug 'digitalis', used in heart disorders, is still derived from the foxglove. Yet again, many flowers played a part as teaching aids by their association with the saints in the conversion of our forebears to Christianity. You will find plenty of these to choose from in the list at the back of this book.

Probably not of much relevant interest to the visitor, but perhaps to us and worth a mention here, is the variation in the common names given to wild flowers, which can be found from country to country. For example, the German name for foxglove is *fingerhut*, or thimble, while the French call it *doigts de la vierge,* the Virgin's fingers.

It seems that mankind is perhaps encouraged to become more 'sophisticated' in his appreciation of beauty. We would certainly not be giving a disservice by reminding people of the incredible beauty of the wild flowers which with no interference or assistance from man continue to lie at our feet.

16
Church
Festivals

Praise, O Praise our God and King;
Hymns of adoration sing;
For His mercies still endure
Ever faithful, ever sure.

Sir H. W. Baker

We all decorate our churches for the various festivals throughout the year: Easter, Whitsun, Christmas, as well as our thanksgiving for harvest; perhaps, too, the patronal festival, the day of the saint to whom the church is dedicated.

One of these festivals might seem an appropriate time to encourage others to come to our church and to share our joy. Probably in the normal scheme of things we have more flowers than usual in the church for a festival. What we are talking about, therefore, is to have even more flowers and at the same time to convey the message of the particular festival we have chosen. It is a fact of life that the three main festivals of Easter, Whitsun and Christmas being holiday times, more people would be likely to visit a flower festival than on an average weekend. In addition, the festival could be extended to include the Bank Holiday Monday, if there was one. What must concern us is that we make their visit worthwhile.

EASTER

The fact that at Eastertime we are celebrating the joy of the risen Christ at the same time as the coming of spring and new life emerging in the natural world, is no coincidence. The name Easter was adapted from the old English *eastre*, a heathen festival held at the vernal equinox (around about 21 March, known to us as the first day of spring). This festival was held in honour of the Teutonic goddess of dawn. The significance in the parallel drawn between the resurrection and the spring flowers and blossoms is obvious, providing a further instance of using flowers and trees as teaching aids, in this case carefully timed to bring home the Easter story. Nothing, therefore, can be more meaningful for Easter decorations than the spring flowers.

In times past Easter Sunday was a time of remembrance and as much, if not more, decorating was done on the graves in the churchyard as was done inside the church itself. In between services great numbers of people walked in the churchyard, viewing the graves and remembering the departed. Judging by Kilvert's account of Easter Sunday, 1870, primroses were particularly popular for grave decorating and were easily come by. Sadly, not so easily found today, but it would be nice to think that there will always be some for our churches on Easter Sunday.

You will undoubtedly have various ideas that you normally use at Easter. It would certainly seem appropriate to have a garden of Gethsemane showing Christ's tomb with the stone rolled away. A lovely place to use primroses and violets and all the little spring flowers. Moss is most useful in making a garden of this nature, but do remember to protect whatever surface you are using it on, with a good strong layer of polythene.

Another visual aid to the Easter story is to have a simple wooden cross, with an arrangement at its foot. Altar crosses are usually ornate and it is not always easy to convey the meaning with flowers on the altar. A floor-standing wooden cross (it need not be enormous) is far more moving in its simplicity and enables the visitor to stand at its foot, as it were. Lilies, or just one lily, could be incorporated in a decoration at the base of the cross. For the main church decorating there are the early flowering blossoms, crab apple, almond and plum, and the shrubs, the daphnes, forsythia and flowering currant. With the red flowering currant I find that if you cut stems and bring them indoors to encourage them to flower early, they tend to produce practically white flowers, which, for Easter, I much prefer, as they blend better with all the lovely yellows and white of the daffodils and narcissi. There is certainly a wealth of flowers and foliage that can be used at Easter. As with all festivals, try to keep the altar flowers white and joyful, giving special significance to the Holy Table.

You may think it is not necessary to have any written aids to the Easter story; everyone is familiar with it. Perhaps what is needed is a reminder of its significance for us. Lines from Easter hymns, or verses from the Bible are always a help, or perhaps the collect for Easter day.

WHITSUN

Whit Sunday falls on the seventh Sunday after Easter when we commemorate the descent of the Holy Spirit upon the disciples on the day of Pentecost when white (whit) clothes were worn.

Traditionally, as well as white flowers, red flowers are used in churches, the latter representing the tongues of flame in which the Holy Spirit descended. The Whitsun colourings do not appeal to me from the aesthetic point of view, but if you have a church that can take them, then they can be really lovely.

If Easter is late you will probably have more flowers to choose from, including flame-coloured 'lily flowering' tulips which can be effective. Because we are using only red and white, in order to create a diversity, as well as using white flowers only on the altar, you could have white flowers only by the chancel steps where the marriage vows are taken, and again round the font where, of course, baptisms take place. Other arrangements can either be a mixture of red and white, or all red. Perhaps you have some steps where you can have a descending arrangement of tongues of flame.

Probably some kind of explanation about Whitsun is called for. Very probably people are not as familiar with its significance as they are with that of Easter and Christmas. The first verse of the hymn

O Joy, because the circling year
Hath brought our day of blessing here!
The day when first the light divine
Upon the church began to shine.

would seem an appropriate one to start with. A little further on the tour round the church could be the first verse from F. C. Burkitt's hymn

Our Lord, His passion ended,
Hath gloriously ascended,
Yet though from Him divided,
He leaves us not unguided:
All His benefits to crown
He hath sent his Spirit down,
Burning like a flame of fire
His disciples to inspire.

Further on again, the verse

Like unto quivering tongues of flame
Upon each one the Spirit came;
Tongues that the earth might hear their call,
And fire, that love might burn in all.

and, finally, perhaps

Spirit of mercy, truth, and love,
O shed thine influence from above
And still from age to age convey
The wonders of this sacred day.

Alternatively, you might prefer R. F. Littledale's translation of that old hymn 'Come down, O Love divine'.

112   *Church Festivals*

CHRISTMAS

In the same way as the adoption of Easter from the heathen festival 'eastre', so Christmas was a take-over of the heathen festival known as the 'winter solstice'. At this festival holly and ivy were used, candles were lit, and the yule log was burned. Nothing has changed, except perhaps for the heating systems in our churches, the yule log now getting burnt in the home hearth!

Katharine McClinton in her *Flower Arrangement in Church* writes:

> The Christmas crib (or creche) has existed in the church since earliest time. Although at one time frowned upon, it was revived by St Francis of Assisi, who received permission from the Pope to construct a crib in the fir woods of Greccio, Italy. St Francis built a rustic stable as a shelter for the nativity scene. He used live models and a live ox and ass. There was a solemn procession before the crib, and then St Francis sang hymns and preached a sermon. Thus was revived a custom which is still prevalent in many countries in both the Anglican and the Roman Catholic Church.

To tell the Christmas story there must be a nativity scene with the figures of Mary and Joseph and, of course, the manger. I would suggest depicting the baby Jesus with tiny white flowers lying, as it were, in the straw. In the festival of winter flowers I mentioned how tiny and delicate looking so many of the hardy winter flowers and shrubs seem to be. Surely very meaningful flowers for the celebration of the birth of the baby Jesus. In our carols we sing about the bleak midwinter and snow falling upon snow. This, of course, is not strictly accurate. The climate of the Holy Land allows flowers to bloom all through the year and, therefore, to surround the stable with flowers and foliage would seem appropriate.

The children of your parish may care to bring toy animals, cows and goats, sheep, donkeys and so on to join the shepherds in adoration of the new-born baby Jesus, with flowers and foliage around them all to add to the joy of the occasion. Another idea for children is for them to bring dolls of other countries dressed in their national costume. This brings home to them, and to all of us, that Jesus came for the whole world and everyone everywhere.

Somewhere in the church must be the three wise men coming from afar and each bearing the gift that symbolises the life of Christ. Gold for kingship: One thinks of winter-flowering jasmin or, if you are very clever, the last of the gold chrysanthemums. Frankincense for worship: frankincense being highly scented, how about the very lovely *Daphne odora, Lonicera purpusii* or *Viburnum fragrans,* or all three! Myrhh for suffering: this, of course, we normally depict with berried holly, the leaves symbolising the crown of thorns and the berries Christ's blood shed for us.

Referring again to Kilvert's diary, this time, 24 December, 1871, he writes,

> When I went down to the church again the clerk and schoolmaster were dressing the outer porch arch. The inner arch was wreathed in one beautiful ivy spray.

In many country churches this practice continues. Ivy denotes 'everlasting life' in Christian symbolism and it would be sad indeed if this tenacious and often despised plant ceased to be used in this simple, charming and meaningful way.

No written explanation is needed for the best loved story in the world, but perhaps you may care to end with a verse. This one is by Bishop Brooks.

> O holy child of Bethlehem
> Descend to us, we pray;
> Cast out our sin, and enter in:
> Be born in us to-day.

HARVEST

The harvest thanksgiving service is not, of course, one which is included in the church's calendar, although the Alternative Service Book does include a couple of suitable sentences. It is our own thanks to God for all the good things around us. Since

it was introduced in the nineteenth century it has remained a
very popular festival and one for which many lovely hymns
have been written. My own favourite is Dean Alford's:

> Come ye thankful people come,
> Raise the song of harvest-home:

A line or two of this hymn here and there around the church
just acts as a reminder of the parallel that Christ in his parables
draws, so many times, between our lives and that of seeds and
plants. In our decorations for harvest we use an abundance of
flowers, fruit, corn and vegetables. Beside a display containing
fruit and vegetables and corn could be the lines

> God our maker, doth provide
> For our wants to be supplied

and on a pew back rest the lines

> We ourselves are God's own field
> Fruit unto his praise to yield

Finally, as you leave the church

> Lord of Harvest, grant that we
> Wholesome grain and pure may be.

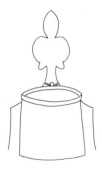

Fig 32

Fig 33 White flowers in candle holders, grapes and bread use the limited space on a small altar table to portray the Communion Service in a simple and meaningful way

A good idea to involve the children, and their parents, is to make small hessian sacks, about 13cm × 15cm (5in × 6in) with wire (coat-hanger wire is excellent) threaded through the hem at the top to keep the mouth open, Then tie the sacks on to your pew ends (Figure 32). The children then each put whatever they like in their own sack. It might be chestnuts or coal or chocolate; flowers, a sugar beet or a bread roll; a jar of jam, a packet of tea, or a pint of milk; firewood or a bunch of herbs. It all makes them, and us, aware of the countless things for which we are saying 'Thank you'.

As we know, Jesus spoke to us in parables, not in deep philosophical terms, but always using everyday examples that could be understood by everyone. So it was when he gave his instructions at the Last Supper. He used symbols that would always be understood – the bread and the wine. Both things for which we give thanks at harvest and surely an ideal opportunity to show them as the body and blood of Christ (Figure 33), in the same way as I suggest portraying the Communion Service, Chapter 7.

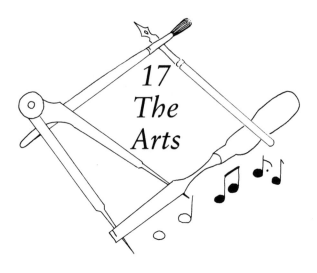

17
The
Arts

Nature I loved, and next to nature art.

Walter Savage Landor

Generally speaking, those talents associated with the arts would come under the headings of

Music	Sculpture
Poetry	Literature
Drama	Painting
Dance	Architecture

It is true to say that so much of what is best in our music, poetry, drama, sculpture, painting and architecture has its roots in our Christian belief. Undoubtedly too a large part of our architectural heritage is in our churches. When seeking ways to portray these various headings, one does not, therefore, have to look very far.

In the first chapter, on the purpose of flowers in church, I touched briefly on the subject of flowers in carvings, stained glass and tapestry hangings. In addition to these were depicted the parables, the sacraments, the life of Christ and so on. These works of art were there to tell a story and act as reminders of Christian beliefs. In this modern age they are possibly forgotten in the light of their original purpose and perhaps a festival, with this theme, would not come amiss.

I am no connoisseur of the arts, and unless you are, liaison with people knowledgeable in these various fields would obviously help enormously. I will, however, attempt to give very obvious examples which you in turn can use to get your point across to the experts!

MUSIC

There are several facets that could be covered here. How many of these you would portray would, of course, depend upon the space available. Firstly songs: the best known songs are undoubtedly songs of praise. Suggestions of hymns and how to interpret them are given in Chapter 4 'Hymns'. Handel's church music would certainly lend itself, and the list of his works must be a long one. A piece written for brass instruments would be well portrayed by lovely gold trumpet lilies. Alternatively, wind instruments could be depicted using reeds, or both could be used together. In opera a combination of orchestra and song – what fun it would be to do Benjamin Britten's *Noye's Fludde*. You could contrive an ark, and then have two each of as many different flowers as you can 'get aboard', perhaps accompanied by a text from Genesis, Chapter 8, verse 22:

> While the earth remaineth, seed-time and harvest,
> and cold and heat, and summer and winter, and day
> and night shall not cease.

Should your organ be suitably placed, then no doubt meaning would be added to 'Music' by siting it in the area of the organ or choir stalls.

POETRY

Rather than repeat myself, I refer you to Chapter 5 'Poetry with Flowers'.

DRAMA

Some of the earliest plays were the miracle plays, depicting stories from the Bible, and surely the most often performed play of all time must be the Nativity play. You could have a Nativity play with a difference, in so far as the characters would be represented by flowers. The Virgin Mary by the Madonna lily and the baby Jesus by white rose buds, both perhaps with a halo of small yellow flowers. In art Joseph is often represented with a budding staff in his hand; he could be represented by the simulation of such a staff. Other groups of flowers could be placed in the scene. The three kings perhaps in gold, the three shepherds, and so on.

One cannot think of drama without thinking of Shakespeare. Possibly more than any other dramatist, time and again Shakespeare mentions flowers, and of course herbs which were such a vital part of Elizabethan life. Born in what was then a very small market town, he would only have been a few minutes' walk from meadows, woods, and the banks of the river Avon. Like so many others before him he chose the familiar flowers to illustrate a point, to draw a parallel and often to describe a character.

When you consider, it is sadly only since the building explosion of houses, factories and roads during this present century, more than any other, resulting in the diminishing acreage of farmland which in turn has led to inflated land prices, that the wild flower population has declined so much. Their usage in everyday expressions has followed suit. In my youth we 'wilted'. The young today are 'shattered'. A trite example perhaps, but nevertheless relevant.

Probably Shakespeare's *The Winter's Tale* and *A Midsummer Night's Dream* contain the greatest number of references to flowers and herbs; certainly some of the better known ones. From the latter:

> I know a bank where the wild thyme blows,
> Where oxslips and the nodding violet grows
> Quite over-canopied with luscious woodbine,
> With sweet musk-roses and with eglantine.

How lovely it would be were you to create such a bank in your church.

From *The Winter's Tale*:

> For you there's rosemary and rue; these keep
> Seeming and savour all the winter long;
> Grace and remembrance be to you both.

If you allow the herbs in your garden to flower, then you will have a considerable amount of colour. However, an arrangement of herbs not in flower is equally attractive. For example, besides rosemary and rue there is the gold marjoram; sages silver, green and gold, and green splashed with red and white; purplish, or sometimes pink and white, thymes; and the dark-leaved fennel, the so-called 'black fennel'.

For an overall quotation for 'Drama' I would choose these lines by Francis Bacon:

> But men must know, that in this theatre of man's life it is reserved only for God and angels to be lookers on.

DANCE

Starting with ballet, immediately three examples from Tchaikovsky spring to mind. *The Sleeping Beauty,* a lovely arrangement of buds perhaps; *Swan Lake,* some feather-like white chrysanthemums or ostrich plume asters, together with shades of blue for the water. 'The Waltz of the Flowers' from *The Nutcracker,* a nice light arrangement, nothing heavy.

Then there is folk dancing, the dancing that is traditional to a particular country or area. Many countries have flowers as emblems or associated with them, so you could select flowers that way. Most of the flowers we grow in our gardens have originated from other countries, therefore, these flowers happily arranged together would be lovely, and it would be of interest too to list the flowers and their country of origin.

For your written word, how about Ecclesiastes, Chapter 3, verses, 1, 2 and 4:

To every *thing there is* a season, and
a time to every purpose under the
heaven:

A time to be born, and a time to
die; a time to plant, and a time to
pluck up *that which is* planted;

A time to weep, and a time to laugh;
a time to mourn, and a time to dance.

SCULPTURE

Very probably you have some form of sculpture in your
church; the most likely might be of the Virgin Mary. White
Madonna lilies, arranged in the simple style of Japanese floral
artists, would be lovely. You might have a sculptured figure of
your patronal saint; ideas for using flowers to represent a
saint, or saints, can be found on page 133. Yet again, you
might have a sculpture of cherubs. There are a great many
flower 'containers' in use which take the form of a cherub
holding up a shallow vessel in which flowers can be arranged.
Some of these, in all honesty, are pretty ghastly, but, as with so
many things, the idea is copied from beautiful objects, like
torchères, for instance. The original would be ideal used in this
context. Very possibly you have a fine font that should have
attention drawn to it. Undoubtedly too you have intricate
stone or wood carving around an archway or over a niche.
These scroll-like carvings frequently depict fruit and flowers:
the lily, the rose, vines and often pomegranates. The latter,
because they have so many seeds within the one fruit, are
representative of the unity of the church. The roses, one is
frequently told, are Tudor roses, and I am sure that in most
cases that is so. Some of them, however, I feel equally sure are
there, as are the lilies, the vines and the pomegranates, as
symbols, or reminders, of their significance in Christian beliefs
(see Chapter 1). For whatever reason the roses are there, they
are there in great numbers. If you make a point of looking, you
might well be surprised at how many you find! The Alternative
Service Book, which is now widely used in the Church of

England, does not include the 'Table to find Easter Day'. As children this table kept us amused if we became bored during the sermon. Perhaps the modern child could amuse itself by counting roses.

Roses then can be complemented with roses, lilies with lilies, vines with grapes and vine leaves, oak leaves with oak leaves, and so on. Oasis sausages for garlands would probably help here.

Many of these carvings in our churches do not, perhaps, receive the attention they deserve. Certainly here is a golden opportunity to draw attention to them, and to give the visitors any information you have on their history, and significance.

LITERATURE

The Bible is undisputedly the best read book there is. Your church will have a lectern with a Bible upon it, so this would seem the obvious choice of site. The Bible is rich in parables, using everyday things and examples to explain a moral or illustrate a point. Because flowers are our means of illustrating our points, then it seems natural to take a quote from the Song of Solomon, Chapter 2, verses 11 and 12,

> For lo the winter is passed and the rain is over and gone. The flowers appear on the earth. The time of the singing of the birds is come.

Or, alternatively, St Matthew, Chapter 6, verses 28 and 29:

> Consider the lilies of the field, how they grow; they toil not, neither do they spin; and yet I say unto you that even Solomon in all his glory was not arrayed like one of these.

Bear in mind that these 'lilies' were not lilies as we understand them, but the wild anemones indigenous to the Holy Land. An arrangement of wild flowers would, therefore, be appropriate. Space permitting, there are obviously plenty of books you could choose as well as the Bible.

PAINTING

This can be approached in several ways and, depending upon the extent of the area available, you might try them all.

Firstly, you may well have a painting in your church that could be complemented, or even emulated, using flowers. Into this category I would also put stained glass. The pictures in these stained-glass windows cover a variety of subjects.Many are of Christ and the Virgin Mary, many others, particularly those in panels, depict biblical stories, others are memorials, and so on. All these can be interpreted with flowers or you may prefer just to complement them either in the colours of your flowers, or by using the same flowers, as often as not the lily, which often appears as a border in a stained-glass window, framing, as it were, the central figure.

Quite another idea would be to have your flower arrangement literally 'framed' in a picture frame. This can be most effective, but do bear in mind that just as an unsuitable frame does not do justice to a painting, so your frame must be of suitable colour and style for your flowers. The flowers in turn should be well balanced within the frame, so that each appears to be part of the other. In addition to using fresh flowers, you could have a painting of dried flowers, or a collage of pressed flowers. To complete your painting exhibition, why not include a framed arrangement of wild flowers, accompanied by these lines from Shakespeare's *Love's Labour's Lost*:

> When daisies pied and violets blue
> And lady-smocks all silver white
> And cuckoo-buds of yellow hue
> Do paint the meadows with delight . . .

These lines would be equally suited to another idea, namely to draw attention to some of the best of the many fine botanical drawings that exist. For example, Keeble Martin's illustrations in his book of wild flowers and the flowers themselves alongside would be interesting as well as attractive.

ARCHITECTURE

Whether you are decorating a cathedral or a tiny village church, and whether the building is centuries old or post-war, I am sure you have a beautiful building of architectural interest. Ceilings, windows, arches, columns, etc can all be drawn attention to and decorated with, or complemented by, flowers. In your 'hand-out' for visitors could be interesting information on the building, together with dates.

It could be that you are fortunate enough to have a 'rose window' – a circular window, traceried to resemble a rose. Such a window would be a very dominant feature in the church and could be reflected on the floor below with a huge circle of flowers, arranged so as to copy exactly the colour and shape of the pattern in the window.

Quite another idea for depicting architecture would be to draw attention to some particularly outstanding local building, or perhaps you are in a county where a particular style of architecture predominates. One of the lovely thatched houses or cottages (many preserved by the National Trust) would be charming with a cottage garden in front. You might prefer something with more architectural significance, such as an Elizabethan manor house with a knot garden; or a monastic building with a herb garden. The buildings in these cases would need to be large photographs, unless of course you have an artist or model maker in your community. Viewing this kind of exhibit would need to be done in perspective, and thus care should be given to the placing of this type of display.

Because the church itself plays such a large part in the interpretation of this theme, you might choose to have one or two verses from W. Bullock and Sir W. H. Baker's hymn, 'We love the place, O God' shown as people enter and leave your festival.

It is the house of prayer,
Wherein Thy servants meet;
And Thou, O Lord, art there
Thy chosen flock to greet.

18
Dried
Flowers

Gardener, if you listen, listen well:
Plant for your winter pleasure, when the months
Dishearten

Vita Sackville West

Nothing could be more welcome in the dreary winter months than to bring summer back into your church for a day, or indeed many days.

The advantages of this theme are obvious. Firstly, you are not competing with every other church in the district. Secondly, you need not worry about your flowers dying, so you could carry on for a whole week and, thirdly, there is less for people to 'do' in the winter and, given good publicity, I am sure you would attract numerous visitors.

There is no reason why you should have 'Dried Flowers' only as your title. You could use many of the suggested themes in this book. How about 'crafts' for example? You could then have a sale of crafts as your second attraction, which would go down well before Christmas. There would always be a sale for your surplus dried flowers, although I am sure that you would not want to part with your more precious ones; however, bunches of *statice, helichrysum* and chinese lanterns sell well. I am not for a moment suggesting that the arrangements should largely be done with these flowers – far from it. If you are going to attract visitors to your festival, then a great deal of work must be put in during the previous year. It is all such delightful and rewarding work, however, that if you do not already dry flowers for your own home use, I am sure you would after you have done it once. My Christmas present list includes as many arrangements as I have dried flowers and time to make. You could do the same and sell them, and also perhaps sell calendars made with pressed flower collages.

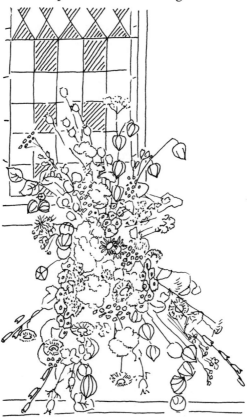

Fig 34 The precipitous slope beneath a stained glass window makes a well lit background for an arrangement of dried flowers whose colours complement the coloured panes

There are many books on drying and preserving flowers and how to treat each individual variety. I am sure your local library could supply some, or if you are 'hooked' and want your own, there are some beautiful and helpful ones to choose from. You might be surprised at the vast range of flowers that can be preserved. The dust cover of the book I use has a lovely arrangement of pink 'Carol' roses, deeper garnette roses, border carnations, pink larkspur, red maple leaves and grasses, and looks as if it had come straight from a June border.

The suggestions on planning and placing, therefore, apply with dried flowers as they do with fresh flowers. The only difference is that because you don't need water, some people might prefer to do the bulk of their arrangement at home. In the case of disabled people this might help, although it would be a pity if they missed the atmosphere and fun of seeing it all 'coming together'. I feel very strongly, however, that with most arrangements, even if for facility of carrying they are begun at home, they should certainly be completed *in situ*. Any arrangement, fresh or dried, brought to a church complete and put into its place looks just like that and never really seems at one with its surroundings. There is no reason why dried flowers should not be arranged exactly as if they were fresh flowers, and the whole effect appear equally natural. I would not choose to have 'swags'. To me they look like Victorian bell-pulls, and as such totally out of place in church. You may well like them, if so, here is your opportunity to make one!

Should you decide to have, say, 'Poetry with Dried Flowers,' or any other title involving the written word, then to have a cartouche made with pressed or dried flowers (stuck firmly on to the cardboard) would be very attractive. The shape of the cartouche could be altered to suit the lines within, and of course the subject matter. It could be circular, oval, heart-shaped, semi-circular, square, oblong or scroll-like. If this is something you have not done, there is a charming book called *Pressed Flower Collages* by Pamela McDowall and published by the Lutterworth Press. It is full of attractive ideas and gives simple and easily followed instructions.

There is no reason why dried or pressed flower cartouches of this nature could not be made for the written words in any of the suggested themes in this book. It is a fascinating pastime and one that could easily involve the housebound person or those in wheelchairs. They could be supplied with material by an active person with an eye for what to press.

These cartouches could be made with pressed flowers in the colourings used for the dried flowers in each particular arrangement and on cards in the palest shade of the predominating colour, thus making the whole colour scheme of flowers, collages and cards complementary.

Like dried flowers, pressed flowers cannot be produced overnight. This whole theme is one which calls for considerable forward planning. However, it is all great fun and very worthwhile.

19
The Church's Year and the Church's Week

The nature of God is a circle, the centre of which is everywhere and the circumference nowhere.

Anon

'Flowers are used as an expression of faith.' To portray the church's year with flowers would, therefore, seem very natural.

The main events in the church's calendar take place in the following order:

Advent	Easter
Christmas	Rogation Sunday
The Epiphany	Ascension Day
Mothering Sunday	Whit Sunday
Palm Sunday	Trinity

This list omits the season of Lent, because, at that time, there would be no flowers in church. To these ten could be added the Harvest Festival and the festival of the Saint or Saints to whom your church is dedicated. This would give you twelve 'headings', as it were. The amount of space allocated to each, and the number of arrangements in each, would depend upon the size of your church.

The placing would need to be worked so that, not only were the various feasts viewed in the correct order, namely as they take place in the church's calendar year, but so that Easter was placed in the sanctuary. One idea might be if you started with Advent under the tower, then Christmas could be around the area of the font. Next would come Epiphany as you started up one side of the nave, followed further up by Mothering Sunday. Palm Sunday could be at the chancel steps leading on to Easter in the sanctuary. The visitor would then turn and retrace his steps passing the vestry where Rogation Sunday could be portrayed. Continuing on the return journey down the chancel steps, the next arrangements would be viewed on the opposite side of the nave to those viewed on the way up. Should the pulpit be conveniently situated on this side, then this would be a splendid place for Ascension Day. Rood-screen steps would be lovely for Whit Sunday. These two sites could well come in the reverse order; this wouldn't matter as one arrangement is ascending and the other descending. As the visitor starts down the nave again, first would come Trinity and then the Harvest Festival. The Saints' day or days could be fitted in wherever they came in the year or alternatively in the side chapels, if you have them, or in the porch.

I think that with this theme it would be essential to have a leaflet for the visitor, guiding him or her through the various seasons in the correct order. Probably a brief explanation, and facts of interest on each would be wise, ensuring that any written words accompanying each arrangement would be more meaningful.

ADVENT

The beginning of the church's year, advent means arrival, especially an important one. The Advent colour for church hangings is purple and possibly an arrangement of flowers in palest mauve through to purple would be appropriate. Flowers in bud would be meaningful. However, to keep them in bud for three to four days would be almost impossible. Delphiniums, of course, still with lots of buds unopened would be one idea.

Being a season of penitence some churches might well not

have flowers during Advent itself. You may think, however, that because it is being portrayed, rather than actually happening, some licence might be permissible.

CHRISTMAS

See page 112.

THE EPIPHANY

See pages 112–13.

MOTHERING SUNDAY

There is nothing new about Mothering Sunday, the fourth Sunday in Lent; it has been celebrated since earliest Christian times. Pre-Reformation it was known as Laetare Sunday, from the Latin rejoice and the purpose was that of rejoicing and thanksgiving for the Christian family and the Church as Mother of us all. In Protestant churches after the Reformation, the Latin name was dropped and the term Mothering Sunday adopted, thus giving a twofold emphasis: rejoicing and thanksgiving for our Mother Church and at the same time remembering and giving thanks for our earthly mothers. It was customary to visit parents on that Sunday and to take presents. Those visiting country parishes would naturally pick the wild flowers as they journeyed homeward along the lanes and in particular they picked violets and took mother a posy and so violets have become emblematic of Mothering Sunday.

Small posies of flowers, with which of course the children could help, would be the obvious choice of flower arrangement. Very possibly windowsills would be the site for Mothering Sunday, and these, well protected, and covered in moss would look lovely with multicoloured posies dotted around and growing, as it were, in the moss. If your sills are flat, you would have to devise a slope, otherwise the flowers would not be seen. Alternatively, should you have a free-standing pillar, conveniently placed, then this could symbolise the Mother Church and the posies could be arranged in a circle on the floor around it and a maypole effect created. Rather than using ribbons to tie the flowers to the 'pole', fix together long pieces of ivy, or use stylax or some other form of everlasting greenery that will not wilt. A very simple arrangement to do, but as is so often the case, effective and meaningful in its simplicity.

PALM SUNDAY

The Sunday before Easter, so called to commemorate Christ's triumphant entry into Jerusalem, when the multitudes strewed the way with palm branches and leaves. Our climate not being conducive to the growing of palms, the willow is recognised as a substitute in this country. An archway of willow branches would certainly be effective and they could be incorporated in any flower arrangement. Because the focal point, through this arch, will be the altar where the flowers will be white, willow green and silver foliage and white flowers would look well. Purple flowers, the colour of Lent hangings, could be included.

EASTER SUNDAY

See page 109.

ROGATION SUNDAY

The word is derived from the Latin *rogare* – to ask. Rogation Sunday, the fifth after Easter, has certainly been observed from the sixth century and for it the first litany was probably compiled. This was said alternately by the minister and the people as they proceeded around the fields asking for God's blessing on the growing crops and the field workers. (Since that first litany its form has of course been altered and added to.) The Monday, Tuesday and Wednesday following Rogation Sunday were observed as solemn days of prayer. Rogation days were called 'Gang Days', (to gang means to go) and similarly the wild flower milkwort was called rogation or gangflower from the custom of tying bunches of these flowers on to poles to be carried by children and others as they proceeded around the fields reciting the litany. Like many flowers, because if its small size, the milkwort looks best growing. It does, however, press extremely well and pressed blue and pink milkwort have been found to keep their colours for many years. Perhaps a collage of pressed milkwort on a round card with the collect for Rogation Sunday written within it would be a suitable accompaniment to your flower arrangement. This arrangement must surely include some fat ears of wheat, oats and barley (saved and dried from the previous harvest), together with a mixture of wild flowers and perhaps flowers with medicinal value. Ornamental vegetables could also be included.

ASCENSION DAY

The day set aside by the Christian churches to commemorate the ascent of our Lord from earth to heaven, and the day when Christ is proclaimed Lord of all life. Ascension Day falls on the Thursday immediately after the three solemn days of prayer following Rogation Sunday and is also known as 'Holy Thursday'.

Being a festival of our Lord, the colour for the hangings on this day would be white. A curving arrangement of white flowers 'ascending' up the pulpit steps and continued so that it rose well above the level of the top of the pulpit, indeed up to the top of the sounding board if you have one, would be lovely. The collect for Ascension Day would be a good written accompaniment.

WHIT SUNDAY

See page 110.

TRINITY SUNDAY

Since the Middle Ages Trinity Sunday, the Sunday following

Whit Sunday, has been observed as a feast in honour of the Trinity. The epistle and gospel used in the Church of England on that day are the same as those in the lectionary of St Jerome. The collect comes from the sacrementary of St Gregory. The gospel comes from St John, Chapter 3, verses 1 to 15. Verse 15 would be one idea for the written word:

> That whosoever believeth in him should not perish, but have everlasting life.

The epistle comes from Revelation, Chapter 4, verses 1 to 11. If you read the whole of that epistle you might decide to emulate its description of heaven in your flower arrangement. Should you do this, then I think you would really need to have the whole of the epistle written out so that the visitor could see the association between flowers and text.

A trinity, of course, means a group of three. In this case, Father, Son and Holy Spirit. You might choose to have three arrangements accompanied by the last verse from the epistle.

> Thou art worthy, O Lord, to receive glory
> and honour and power: for thou hast created
> all things, and for thy pleasure they are and
> were created.

Trillium grandiflorum with its three sepals and three petals is known as the Trinity Flower. Clover, belonging to the species trifolium (having leaves of three leaflets), is reputed to have been picked by St Patrick to explain to his followers how there could be three Gods in one. It is interesting how often these little instances of the use of flowers as teaching aids in Christian education crop up; perhaps we could copy them.

SAINTS' DAYS

Because there are so many different dedications to our churches, one can only give a general outline of ideas as to how you could depict your patronal saint, or saints, using flowers.

Firstly, I think I would look to the list of saints and their flowers and see if you can get some idea that way. A short history on your saint, included in your hand-out, wouldn't go amiss; that too might produce an idea for the flower side. Again, the colour for saints is white, unless they were martyrs, in which case it is red. That could help you with the colouring of your flowers. If you still have no lead, you could explore the patronage of your saint. For example, St Luke is the patron saint of doctors, so flowers with medicinal properties would be an idea. St Cecilia is the patron saint of music, particularly church music, St Joseph of carpenters, St Peter of fishermen. As with all these themes, once you start ferreting out information, you will find that you will stumble, sooner or later, on an idea.

THE CHURCH'S WEEK

In a small church you might not be able to accommodate the 'Church's Year', in which case you might prefer the 'Church's Week'. Often parishes have set days for particular groups to meet. The idea would be to portray a different activity for each day of the week. The Choir, the Confirmation Class, the Bell-ringers, the Bible Reading Fellowship, the Mothers' Union, the PCC (a little poetic licence here!) and the Sunday School.

The placing of these activities should not be difficult. The Choir would be in the choirstalls, or if you don't have any, around the organ: the Sunday School probably in the nave; the Confirmation Class in the sanctuary; the Bell-ringers under the belltower; the Bible Reading Fellowship in the area of the lectern. The PCC would be in the porch, which was more than likely built to house such gatherings and to transact such business. The Mothers' Union could have the area around the font. Each group would have a flower arrangement and a text in keeping with their particular activity. These could be done in ways already touched upon in other chapters.

These groups all contribute to the church's year and as contributors are very much a part of it. Should your large church have room to combine the two ideas, you would certainly have a most interesting festival.

20
Things of Joy

Creator of the world to Thee
An endless rest of joy belongs

(from an old translation)

The last chapter in any book must surely be the gathering together of thoughts and ideas, and the tying of them together under one heading. To me, the theme 'Things of Joy' does just that.

We used this title for a very successful flower festival many years ago and it certainly was a particularly happy one. Typed hand-outs were given to visitors as they came into the church for them to read and afterwards take home. They began as follows:

> We feel there is no more suitable place to remind ourselves, and you, of the many 'things of joy' which perhaps we take rather too much for granted.
>
> Not only all the joys of family and friends, of sight and sound, of health and comfort, of the arts and of nature, but of the Church itself, and the abundant love of God.
>
> We have tried to express these thoughts through the joy of flowers.

Having said that, it was therefore only necessary to have headings, beautifully written in black script, on white card. These are the headings we used:

Music	See 'Hymns' Chapter 4 or 'The Arts' Chapter 17.
Leisure	An arrangement using wild flowers would indicate this well.
Hearing	Trumpets, or bell-like flowers and reeds, possibly by the organ, would be one idea.
Sleep	An arrangement of seed heads. If this is something you have not done before, you might be surprised how lovely they can be.
Holy Communion	See 'Church Services' Chapter 7.
Health	A particularly rosy looking fresh arrangement.
Sight	Simply a beautiful arrangement of flowers.
Friendship	A mixture of flowers together with some flowering shrubs and foliage.
Childhood	Wherever possible, I think it is important to let the children participate in your festival. Being a very small population, we have very few children, and at the time of this festival only one little girl. She brought her teddy bear and made a daisy chain which she put round his neck. He sat in a pew wearing his daisy chain and hardly needed his 'Childhood' notice beside him. Despite all the years that have passed since then friends still remark how they will never forget that teddy sitting there, wearing his daisy chain and saying so much in such a simple way.
Love	White flowers on your altar will say this for you.
Prayer	An arrangement on a prayer desk.
Knowledge	This one went on the lectern.

Family	A good way to indicate this would be an arrangement of as many different colours of one particular flower as you could muster. Roses for example, or carnations, or aquilegias.
Warmth	I remember this one well. A lovely bright arrangement of oranges and reds with flames of montbretia and red hot pokers set in a dead bark base with puffs of old man's beard for smoke.
Light	A yellow and gold arrangement placed in a candle bracket or lamp standard, or around an electric light bracket on a wall easily makes this point.
Baptism	An arrangement of tiny blue, pink and white flowers round the font base.
Water	A nice flowing blue and white arrangement down your rood screen steps.
Nature	Having already used wild flowers, perhaps you could interpret this with corn and berries and fruits.
Giving	A basket of flowers.
Work	Today one might think to add this title. A farming scene, a vegetable garden, or what you will.

As well as these headings, you could select as many others as you have room for from the chapters on 'The Arts', 'Crafts', or indeed from any of the other themes that may appeal to you.

The hand-out ended, as this book now does, with these words:

In these days of world wide problems and worries, by sharing our joy with you, we hope to give you pleasure to take away with you and to share with others.

The church door closes with Figure 35 overleaf.

Fig 35 A corn cross tied to the wrought iron gate at the entrance to this chapel is equally effective viewed from the other side; leaving the departing visitor with the image of this simply contrived Christian symbol

Conclusion

It is inevitable, when writing a book of this nature, to categorise and suggest a particular approach. My hope is that you will look on this book as a store-cupboard of ideas. There is no need to follow any particular recipe, take out what you fancy from whatever shelf you like; put the ingredients together and make your own special concoction as suits your particular need. I am sure that you will create something very lovely. How can it be otherwise when each and every flower and blossom we use is so very perfect, recalling man's most ancient belief, that God and nature are one.

Appendices

A Table of Liturgical Colours According to the Ancient Use of the Church of England

Advent	Red or Blue
Christmas	Best, otherwise White
St Stephen	Red
St John Evangelist	White
Holy Innocents	Red
During the octaves of Christmas	White
Circumcision	White, or White and Red together
The Epiphany	Best, or otherwise Red or White
During the octave	Red or White
Sundays after Epiphany	Red, or any old or worn vestments or frontals of whatever colour
Septuagesima to Lent	Red or Blue
Ash Wednesday	Red
Weekdays in Lent until Passion Sunday	Plain White, or unbleached linen. The vestments, frontals, and hangings may be adorned with small red, blue or black crosses and other symbols of the Passion.
Sundays in Lent until Passion Sunday	Plain White. Where there is no White, Red or Blue may be used
Passiontide Sundays and weekdays alike	Red. Where more than one set of Red is available, the darker or plainer should be used.
Maundy Thursday	Red
Good Friday	Red vestments at the ante-Communion Service
Easter Even	Red vestments at the ante-Communion Service. At Evensong the Lenten veils still remain up, but the altar hangings and copes should be the Best; otherwise White.
Easter Day	Best, otherwise White. Before the first service of Easter Morning all the Lenten veils and hangings are removed.
Monday and Tuesday in Easter Week	White

The rest of Eastertide	White
Rogation Days	White
Ascension Day	Best, otherwise White
Then till Whit Sunday	White
Whit Sunday	Best, otherwise White. Red was used in a few places.
The rest of Whit week	White or Red
Trinity Sunday	Best, otherwise White or Red
During the week	White or Red
Corpus Christi	Best, otherwise Red, or White and Red together
Sundays after Trinity	Red. Green is ordered in one or two places. The older and less handsome vestments may be used, whatever the colour.
Weekdays after Trinity	As on Sundays
Dedication Festival	Best, otherwise White
The Feast of the Place, the Saint, or Mystery in whose name the Church is dedicated	Best, otherwise those of the colour appropriate to the saint or mystery
Feasts of the Blessed Virgin Mary	White
Saint's Day in Eastertide	White
Apostles, Martyrs and Evangelists, out of Eastertide	Red
Virgin Martyrs	White, or White and Red together
Virgins not Martyrs	White
Confessors	Yellow, Green or Blue. If the Church possesses sets of each of these colours, Green may be reserved for doctors and bishops, blue for ascetic and monastic confessors, and Yellow for the rest.
Holy Matrons	Yellow or Green
Angels	White or Red
Holy Cross Days (even in Eastertide)	Red
Nativity of St John Baptist	White or Blue
St Mary Magdalene	White, Green and Yellow, Yellow, or Blue
The Transfiguration	White (no English medieval information)

The Holy Name	Best, otherwise Red
All Saints' Day	Best, otherwise Red and White together
All Souls' Day	Black, or Blue in default of Black
Funerals and Requiem	
Services	Black, or dark Blue
Baptisms	Red
Confirmations	Red
Weddings	Green, Red or Blue
Votive Services:	
For Peace	White
For Thanksgiving	Best, otherwise Red or White
For the Parish	Red or Blue

Old English Table of Flowers

Nov.	30	St Andrew	Three-coloured wood sorrel
Dec.	6	St Nicholas	Nest-flowered heath
	8	Conception of Blessed Virgin Mary	Arbor vitae
	13	St Lucy	Cypress arbor vitae
	16	O. Sapientia	Chinese arbor vitae
	21	St Thomas	Sparrow wort
	25	Christmas	Madonna lily
	26	St Stephen	Purple heath
	27	St John Evangelist	Flame heath
	28	Innocents	Bloody heath, rosebuds
	31	St Silvester	Pontieva
Jan.	1	Circumcision	Laurustinus
	6	Epiphany	Screw moss
	8	St Lucian	Yellow tremella
	13	St Hilary	Yew tree
	18	St Prisca	Four-toothed moss
	20	St Fabian	Large dead-nettle
	21	St Agnes	Christmas rose
	22	St Vincent	Early whitlow grass
	25	Conversion of St Paul	Christmas rose
Feb.	2	Purification Blessed Virgin Mary	Snowdrop, box
	3	St Blasius	Great watermoss
	5	St Agatha	Common primrose
	14	St Valentine	Crocus, early primrose
	24	St Matthias	Great fern
Mar.	1	St David	Leek, daffodil

	2	St Chad	Dwarf cerastium
	7	St Perpetua	Early daffodil
	12	St Gregory	Chamelled ixia
	18	St Edward	Great leopard bane
	21	St Benedict	Bulbous fumitory
	25	Annunciation Blessed Virgin Mary	Madonna lily, daffodil, marigold, white iris, narcissus, almond blossom, Our Lady's smock
Apr.	3	St Richard	Evergreen alkanet
	4	St Ambrose	Red crown imperial
	19	St Alphege	Wisine garlic
	23	St George	Red and white roses, harebell
	25	St Mark	Clarimond tulip
May	1	St Philip and St James	Tulip, St James' red campion, red bachelor's buttons
	3	Invention of the Cross	Poetic narcissus, crowsfoot, ranunculus
	6	St John before the Latin Gate	*Lucken gowans*, Latin (garden daisy, dandelion, marigold)
	19	St Dunstan	Monk's hood
	26	St Augustine	Canterbury bell
	27	Venerable Bede	Yellow bachelor's buttons
June	1	St Nicomede	Yellow rose
	5	St Boniface	Three-leaved rose
	11	St Barnabas	Midsummer daisy, ragged robin.
	17	St Alban	Monkey flowers (figroot)
	20	Translation of St Edward	Doubtful poppy, crown's imperial lily
	24	St John Baptist	St John's wort, scarlet campion
	29	St Peter	Yellow rattle
July	2	Visitation of Blessed Virgin Mary	Madonna lily, red and white roses thrift, Our Lady's slipper
	4	Transfiguration of St Martin	Copper day lily
	15	St Swithun	Small cape marigold
	20	St Margaret	Marguerite, poppies, Virginian dragon's head
	22	St Mary Magdalene	Blush rose, African lily (Agapanthus)
	25	St James	Herb Christopher (baneberry,

			flowering fern, fleabane, meadowsweet)
	26	St Anne	Field camomile
Aug.	1	Lammas	Corn, stramony, camomile
	6	Transfiguration	Meadow saffron
	7	Name of Jesus	Common amaranth (love-lies-bleeding)
	10	St Lawrence	Common balsam
	15	Falling asleep of Blessed Virgin Mary	Rosemary, lavender, virgin's bower (wild clematis), roses, lilies.
	24	St Bartholomew	Sunflower
	28	St Augustine	Goldenrod
	29	St John Baptist beheaded	Yellow hollyhock
Sept.	1	St Giles	Great sedum (stonecrop)
	7	St Evurtius	Golden starwort (aster family)
	8	Nativity of Blessed Virgin Mary	Aster or daisy
	14	Holy Cross	Passion Flower
	17	St Lambert	Narrow-leaved mallow
	21	St Matthew	Cilcated passion flower
	26	St Cyprian	Gigantic goldenrod
	29	St Michael and All Angels	Michaelmas daisy
	30	St Jerome	Golden amaryllis
Oct.	1	St Remigius	Lowly amaryllis
	6	St Faith	Late-flowering fever-few (Pyrethrum)
	9	St Denys	Milky agaric (Mushroom)
	13	Translation of King Edward	Smooth helenium (sneezeweed)
	17	St Etheldreda	Ten-leaved sunflower
	18	St Luke	Floccose agaric
	25	St Crispin	Fleabane starwort (aster family)
	28	St Simon and St Jude	Late chrysanthemum, scattered starwort dedicated to St Jude
Nov.	1	All Saints	Chrysanthemum, laurustinus
	6	St Leonard	Yew
	11	St Martin	Weymouth pine
	13	St Britius	Bay
	15	St Machutus	Sweet coltsfoot

17	St Hugh	Tree stramony
20	St Edmund	Red stapelia (milkweed family)
22	St Cecilia	Trumpet-flowered wood sorrel, roses
23	St Clement	Convex wood-sorrel
25	St Catherine	Evergreen laurel, sweet butterbur (coltsfoot)

Bibliography

Day, The Rev Ernest Hermitage. *The Sacristan's Handbook* (A. R. Mowbray, 1931)

Day, Lewis F. *Nature in Ornament* 3rd ed (B. T. Batsford, 1896)

Dearmer, The Rev Percy. *The Parson's Handbook,* 12th ed (Humphrey Milford, 1932)

Evans, Ivor H., ed. *Brewer's Dictionary of Phrase and Fable,* Centenary ed (Cassell, 1970)

Felton, R. F. *British Floral Decoration* (Adam and Charles Black, 1910)

Hook, Dr Walter Farquar. *The Church Dictionary,* 11th ed. (John Murray, 1971)

Hooker and others. *Aids to Bible Students (Indices, Concordance etc)* (Society for Promoting Christian Knowledge, ?1875)

Jones, Herbert. *Altar Flowers and How to Grow Them* (R. & T. Washbourne, 1914)

Kerr, Jessica. *Shakespeare's Flowers* (Longman's Young Books, ?1969)

McClinton, Katharine Morrison. *Flower Arrangement in Church* (World's Work, 1957)

Parker, Sir William. *History of Long Melford.* (1873) Roger Martyn's description of Long Melford Church before the Reformation.

Perry, Frances. *Flowers of the World* (Hamlyn, 1972)

Plomer, William, ed. *Kilvert's Diary* (Jonathan Cape, 1939/40)

Quennell, C. H. B. and Marjorie. *A History of Everyday Things in England* (B. T. Batsford, 1919)

Rankin, M. M. *Wild Flowers* (Andrew Melrose, 1909)

The Reader's Digest Book of Herbs. (The Reader's Digest, 1971)

Taylor, Gladys. *Saints and their Flowers* (A. R. Mowbray, 1956)